BELIE

Start living the life you have always dreamed of. Today.

Adrian Falk

Other authors, whose works have been mentioned or quoted in this publication, have been acknowledged at the end of this book.

Disclaimer: This book is not intended as a substitute for the medical advice of physicians. The content is of the nature of general comment only and is not in any way recommended as individual advice. The reader should regularly consult a physician in matters relating to his/her health and particularly with respect to any symptoms that may require diagnosis or medical attention.

www.believeadvertising.com

Paperback ISBN: 978-0-6486660-2-8
eBook ISBN: 978-0-6486660-8-0

This book is dedicated to everyone who never believed in me.
Thank you for being my motivation to prove you wrong in my life.

Table of Contents

It's time to start believing

Y

ou wake up one Saturday morning, thinking to yourself: *Why am I so ordinary? Why can't I be remarkable like others? Why can't I be out of this world?*

Sounds familiar?

Of course it does.

Millions of people all across planet earth awake to these very same thoughts on many a Saturday.

So, what seems to be the issue then?

The early summer sun is bathing your bedroom in a golden glow, the smell of freshly mowed lawns fills your senses, the sound of children laughing in the park rings in your ears and a beautiful yellow-and-black bird is perched on the windowsill outside your bedroom.

Everything *around* you seems to be pitch perfect and, yet, everything *inside* of you feels crooked.

You climb out of bed and look at yourself in the mirror.

Good grief, I have gained so much weight! your mind tells you. *I really should do something about it.*

Since you have nothing planned for the day, you dress in your oldest clothes and walk into the kitchen to make some coffee to clear your blurry mind.

You check your phone but there is nothing interesting happening on social media.

When is anything exciting ever going to happen in my life? you think, switching on the television. You flip through the channels and notice all those successful people, being portrayed by actors. The coffee tastes bad and the caffeine is making you jumpy.

You switch off the television, sighing. *Why on earth am I so incredibly ordinary? I don't want to be ordinary, I want to be great.*

The important question now becomes: How do you change this around?

How do you transform yourself from an ordinary human being into something special; something great? How do you achieve those goals you have always dreamed about?

The answer is not that difficult. In fact, it boils down to a single word:

BELIEVE.

Little voices in the back of your head keep on saying that you will never be great, that you will never be awesome. Shut them out. Put them aside. Do whatever you have to do to make them stop. These voices are your worst enemy.

Your friend is your soul. Because your soul can counter these voices by saying, "I am what I choose to be."

* * *

This book is to assure you that you can achieve what you've always dreamed of, you just have to believe in yourself.

We all have struggles in some way, shape or form, but with creative visualisation and self-belief, you will be able to manifest what you have always wanted.

Ask yourself the right questions about your destiny and you will come up with the answers. They are all in there; you only have to unlock them.

We are sometimes too afraid of change. But, if the change is for the better it should give us joy, right?

That's the crux of the problem.

We doubt whether the change is going to be for the better and really bring joy to our lives. This doubt then causes us to shy away from change, prohibiting us to see the other side of the world; the side where our dreams lie.

Then we never get to open the door to happiness…

My name is Adrian Falk and I will assist you in reaching your goals and dreams.

Can we make the trip to greatness together?

Can I lead you to waking up on a Saturday morning, believing in yourself one hundred per cent?

Let us find out.

Read these chapters and you might finally become the ruler of your own universe.

Before you read further, clear your mind and let harmony wash over your inner self.

CHAPTER 1

How to live the life you want when no one else believes in you…

S

o, how do I achieve this? Once again, the answer is not that difficult. You have to put everything around you aside and focus on your inner self for a change. Stop worrying about the outside world and start to put the emphasis on *yourself*.

"Wait," you might say, "what about my wife, my husband, my boyfriend, my girlfriend, my children?"

The crux of the matter is the other way around: once you have effected a change in *yourself*, it will automatically bring you closer to your loved ones.

This change can only happen with self-belief, even if you don't feel up to the challenge from the outset. Remember this: only *you* can make positive changes to yourself. Nobody else.

The great Mahatma Gandhi once said, "If I have the belief that I can do it, I shall surely acquire the capacity to do it, even if I may not have it at the beginning."

Adrian Falk with Novak Djokovic

This is so very true, I found out at a very early stage of my life here on earth.

At age twenty, I moved from Sydney to New York City (when no one said I could) and worked in my dream job in advertising and public relations for three years. During that time, I rubbed shoulders with the rich and famous and was invited to various A-list, red carpet events.

Although it was quite an exciting time in my life, I wanted more. I wanted to be more independent and call the shots instead of waiting for someone else to do so.

Upon moving back to Australia, when I was twenty-four years old, I started my own business. Once again, nobody – not even my friends and family – believed that I could make a success out of it, but I did.

I have now been operating in my own company, *Believe Advertising and PR*, for seventeen years and have worked with many national and international brands, including sporting heroes such as Novak Djokovic.

How did I do it?

By applying pure self-belief, that's how.

I really believe in the powers of the mind. Great hidden powers that can bring about so much change it becomes alarming – but in a good way.

Employing the right mindset to achieve what you want in life is just one of these powers.

The dilemma is that very few people know how to exploit the power of the mind.

Therefore, I have developed a ten-step plan anybody can follow to develop and enrich their mind-power.

Each one of these steps will be covered in a different chapter of the book but here they are, in case you want to ponder on them in the meantime:

ONE: Take a deep breath.

TWO: Be grateful

THREE: Take action

FOUR: Confront negative influences

FIVE: Have a vision

SIX: Mind your thoughts

SEVEN: Take time to reflect

EIGHT: Give back

NINE: Find support

TEN: Believe!

No matter what your goals, dreams or life-plan, these ten steps will assist you in successfully achieving the end result.

See this list as a recipe for success.

The ten ingredients are ten different ways of accomplishing victory in different aspects of life.

And remember, the recipe can be re-used.

Some people might have one goal, for instance: financial independence. Others might have a multitude of dreams, like building the perfect relationship, or achieving spiritual enlightenment, or even simple tasks like passing grade eleven, or acing their fourth year at university to obtain a post-graduate degree.

All of this can be achieved by applying the recipe, but you have to know how and when to use the ingredients in order to make a success.

If you use these ten steps, you will finally be able to live the life you've always wanted to live, even if a lot of other people don't believe in you.

Why? Because with a strong sense of self-belief you won't need too many other people to believe in you.

Before you continue with this journey, I would like you to think about your goals and dreams in life. Focus on one or two, or even three, and begin to apply the recipe's ten steps to success to each one of them.

You will also notice that, unlike in a cookbook, this recipe has no quantities attached to the ingredients. The names of the ingredients are there, but there is (for the moment) no indication of how much you should use.

This is intentional, due to the fact that the recipe is not cast in stone.

Some goals – like building a relationship – will require a greater dosage of step eight (give back) while others – like financial independence – will require a substantial amount of step three (take action).

Let us start our voyage by dissecting the recipe…

CHAPTER 2

Take a deep breath

This is the twenty-first century. Nothing happens at a slow pace anymore. Drones are flying around, cell phones are buzzing and many people are ruled by the pressure of social media. Life is a never-ending rush of wake up, drive to work or school, slave the day away, drive home, make dinner, eat dinner, watch television, sleep, and then repeat.

It doesn't have to be like that, you know?

A good twenty-minute-a-day timeout can do wonders for the soul and can sometimes be just as effective in relaxing the mind as a two-week holiday.

So, how about this? Go to bed twenty minutes earlier every night and allow yourself to get up twenty minutes earlier every morning. Then use these first twenty minutes of each day to walk out into the fresh morning air. Whether it's into a hazy shade of winter or into a bright sunny summer day, walk outside and apply the following four rules:

- Leave your cell phone on the kitchen table.
- Do not switch on the television.

- Do not listen to any music.
- Do not read anything.

No more distractions, okay?

Are you ready?

Let's go.

Suck in a generous amount of oxygen and nitrogen (provided to us free of charge by Mother Earth) and clear your mind.

Deep breathing is a major part of your personal well-being. The more you breathe, the more you will prosper. You don't have to force yourself to breathe; it happens automatically. But you can force yourself to breathe *more* and *deeper*. This will allow your metabolism to increase, making clarity of the mind easier.

Now, use your twenty early morning minutes to breathe and to contemplate.

Think about your life in silence. Think about your goals. Think about believing in yourself.

It doesn't matter whether your thoughts are about kicking a bad habit such as smoking or taking up a new difficult sport such as archery. Your approach should always be the same: *I believe I can do it!*

Imprint this notion firmly into your mind like a stamp of approval: *I believe I can do it!*

Take your twenty minutes every morning to breathe, clear your head, and fill it with positive thoughts.

"Yes, I hear you, Adrian," you might say, "but what if my brain does not want to play along?"

Not a problem. Studies show that many people cannot *believe* in something they cannot *see* or *hear*. It will be fairly difficult for you to *see* a goal you haven't achieved yet (more on this in Chapter 6 – Have a vision) but let us concentrate on the *hear* part.

Do it then. Say it aloud: "I believe in myself and I believe I can do this." Say it to the bird on the windowsill, say it to the trees, to the lawn or to the patio tiles beneath your shoes. And while you say it, become a dreamer.

If we had no dreamers in the world, we wouldn't have the lightbulb, the train, penicillin, sonar, x-rays, the motorcar, the fax machine, the internet, email, drones, smartphones or 4K television.

The idea behind these twenty early morning minutes is to breathe, think and become a positive dreamer; an optimistic soul-searcher. Don't limit your dreams. Dream as extreme, as big, as profuse, as impossible, as crazy as you want to.

After reading that, you might come back and say, "Adrian, I have tried your twenty minutes, but all my mind comes up with is 'It's too difficult, there are too many obstacles'."

This is perfectly normal. Unfortunately, obstacles always come to mind first. That's the way the human race has been conditioned in today's day and age.

But, don't worry, there is hope.

Just like objects appear to be larger than they are in the rear view mirror, obstacles always appear to be more difficult than they are in the human mind.

For example: when a nine-year-old girl decides to sell homemade lemonade for extra pocket money, she first of all worries about a fold-up table, then about change for her customers, then about where she is going to get enough paper cups, then about whether customers will actually buy her lemonade, and the list goes on…

However, before she knows it, her father has organised the table, her mother has spread the word about her lemonade stand around the neighbourhood, her friends have gathered some coins for change, her uncle has found a hundred paper cups he hadn't used at his thirtieth birthday party the previous year and everything is suddenly sorted.

Always remember this: eighty-five percent of potential problems we worry about will never even materialise. Sometimes our thoughts are trapping us and boxing us in because we focus on the negative.

So, focus the energy of your brain on the positive. *I am going to make this work. I am in control of my life. I WILL make a success out of this.*

Now, take another deep breath.

The author, Douglas Adams, had a nice take on this when he wrote: Don't spin your wheels and stress. Take a deep breath, center yourself and make a plan.

Are you relaxed?

Does the task at hand seem more achievable now?

Good. Let us move on then…

While taking these deep breaths, let us pause for a moment to analyse the letters of the word BELIEVE:

B – Boldness
E – Efficiency
L – Learning
I – Intelligence
E – Endurance
V – Vigilance
E – Equity

This might feel like a cliché to many people, but allow me to show you why it is important.

In order to use the power of your brain successfully, you have to keep these positive words in mind.

Be **bold**. Once you believe you can achieve your goals, you have to sustain the self-assurance that you will succeed.

Be **efficient**. No ambition has ever been reached by being lazy or sluggish. Chase your dreams like you have chased nothing ever before.

Learn from your mistakes and improve on them. If you have, for instance, a goal of losing ten kilograms in one week and you realise on Sunday that you've only lost four, the lesson learnt is that you aimed too high – that it would be impossible to lose so much weight without starving yourself to death. Break your goal down into smaller milestones: five kilograms in week 1 and five in week 2, for example.

That goes hand in hand with **intelligence**. You have to be smart about setting your goals. Challenge yourself, but don't make it ridiculous.

Endurance is probably the most important concept in this list of inspiring words. No great achievement has ever been completed by giving up.

Be **vigilant**. Watchfulness is a key part of reaching your dreams. Observe your progress, observe the changes around you and make adjustments where necessary.

Fair play will enhance the chances of achieving your goals tremendously. You might get away with ignoring **equity** the first time and still complete your achievement, but in the long run, trampling on others will catch up with you.

Take another deep breath.

Now that you have spent your twenty minutes, you can begin to live a better life and you can start to do the things that you want to do in life.

Let that thought linger in your mind throughout the day and repeat your twenty-minute alone time routine tomorrow morning.

It all starts right here and now.

I believe in myself and I will live the life that I desire.

You have just made a step in the right direction. You began the day with a positive affirmation.

My personal positive affirmation came when I was twenty years old.

Growing up, I was one of three kids, the only boy, with middle-child syndrome. Sandwiched between a younger sister and an older sister, whatever I tried to do never felt like it was good enough for my parents. I also wasn't a popular boy at school and, comparing myself to my classmates, always felt unworthy. I guess these factors became kind of bittersweet for me later in life, because I always felt like the underdog.

I wasn't very good at sports but I absolutely loved music. However, my parents told me there would be no proper career for me in music. My one strength was creativeness and that's how I ended up in the advertising business – I thought I could write music for television ads.

While watching a movie called *Muriel's Wedding* when I was in high school, I instantly associated with Muriel Heslop, the socially awkward underdog. Everyone kept on telling her she wouldn't make a success of her life, just like many people had insinuated about mine.

So, when I moved to New York City at the age of twenty, making something big of my life was basically a slap in the faces of those people who didn't believe I could do it.

Joan of Arc once said, "One life is all we have and we live it as we believe in living it. But to sacrifice what you are and to live without belief, that is a fate more terrible than dying."

I couldn't agree with her more. We only have one life. You don't want to make this one life ordinary; you want it to be an extraordinary experience.

Imagine you had a generous donor who deposited $1,440 into a bank account every morning at 00:00 a.m.

Now visualise this account as a special one. You cannot transfer money from this account to another. It carries over no balance from day to day and every night at 11:59 p.m. the account is cleared out – set back to zero – only to be topped up to $1,440 again by your mysterious donor a minute later, at 00:00 a.m.

What will be your first action when you wake up each morning?

You will go to the ATM down the road and draw out every single dollar!

Well, guess what? We all have such a donor and such a bank account. The donor's name is Mother Earth and the account is called Time.

Every morning at exactly 00:00 a.m. the donor credits you with 1,440 minutes.

If you don't use these minutes wisely, the donor will clear them just after 11:59 p.m. and grant you with an equal number of minutes for the following day. However, the previous minutes have now been lost. Time is not a savings account, it is an operational account. There is no overdraft facility and you cannot take out any loans.

So, use your time wisely, breathe deeply and believe you can spend every minute of every day productively.

You have used the first 20 minutes of the day by making a positive affirmation. The question is: What are you going to do with the remaining 1,420 minutes?

Here is my suggestion: spend them positively.

Do not waste any time by filling your mind with negative thoughts.

My perception of time has always been that we can speed it up or slow it down with our actions; even move ahead of time through positive thoughts or lag behind with negative thoughts.

A psychology professor with a glass of water in her hand once asked her students, "How heavy is this glass of water I am holding?"

The students started guessing and shouting out answers when she hushed them by saying, "The absolute weight of this glass of water is of no concern. The perceptual weight is what matters and that depends on how long I hold it. If I hold it for a minute or two, it is pretty light. If I hold it for an hour, its weight might make my arm become numb. And if I hold it for a full day, my arm will cramp up and become paralysed, compelling me to drop the glass to the floor."

Negative thoughts can have a similar effect.

If you think about your worries for a short while, nothing significant should happen. If you think about them for a longer period, your head will probably start to ache and anxiety will set in. And if you think about your worries all day long, you will most likely end up not being able to do anything else until you have dropped the negative thoughts.

Now, consider the question again: What are you going to do with the remaining 1,420 minutes of each day?

CHAPTER 3

Be grateful

Before we continue on the journey to excellence, let us stop for a moment to be thankful for what we have.

There are simply too many things in life that are taken for granted:

Friends and companions, a home to live in, a bed to sleep in, food, fresh water, clothing, technology, books, music, art, education, the internet, transport, mobile phones, trees, rainbows, birds and animals, mountains, sunsets, laughter, the ocean, safety, freedom, electricity, good health, money, hope, the moon and stars, sunrises, forgiveness, our senses, a career, conversations, air to breathe, time…

And the list goes on. I can fill the entire book if I continue to think about everything we have to be grateful for.

Now that you have started to believe in yourself, you also have to believe in gratitude.

"Why?" you might ask. "What does that have to do with me achieving my goals and dreams?"

The answer is *everything*.

Let me give you a few examples:

Say, for instance, your goal is to lose some weight – plus gain some muscle in the process – and you join a local gym in order to help you achieve this.

Number one: be grateful for the actual gym building and its equipment, otherwise you would have had to make another plan at home.

Number two: be thankful for good health, otherwise you might have been too weak to go to the gym.

Number three: be grateful for having the funds to pay the gym's monthly instalments.

Number four: be thankful for a job, otherwise you wouldn't have had the income to provide these funds.

Number five: be grateful for clothes you wear to the gym.

Number six: transport to and from the gym.

Number seven: gym instructors. Number eight: electricity to provide lights inside the gym. Number nine: fresh water to drink after your workout. Number ten: good eyesight to monitor your progress.

Number eleven: nutritious food to give you the strength to perform these workouts. Number twelve: a sound brain to understand the routines in your workout. And number thirteen: fully functioning motor neurons to execute these routines.

And there you were, thinking about one goal while there are thirteen things to be grateful for in trying to achieve that goal. Frightening, right?

Let's test something else.

You just graduated from law school and your goal is to leave your childhood home and become personally and financially independent within two years. How many underlying things are there to be grateful for in achieving this simple task?

Go on, write them down:

1. Parents
2. A home to grow up in
3. Primary education
4. Secondary education
5. Tertiary education
6. University professors
7. University buildings
8. The country's laws
9. Law firms
10. Your salary
11. Transport to and from work
12. Electricity
13. …

I'm sure you can think of many more.

The point I am trying to bring across is this: While believing in yourself and believing in your abilities to reach your dreams, there will always be dozens of things to be thankful for as you embark on your journey.

Sometimes these gratitudes come in shapes we never even think about. Here, I'm talking about things that have been taken for granted for so long that we almost expect them as a given.

For example, we expect it as a given that someone will serve us when we sit down at a restaurant table. Granted: we say thank you to the person serving us, but do we say it from the bottom of our hearts? Probably not always.

Way back when, in the days when an ice cream sundae cost much less than today, a seven-year-old boy walked into a coffee shop and sat down at a table. A waitress approached him and asked him what he would like to order.

Studying the mouth-watering ice cream pictures on the board above the coffee counter behind her, he asked, "How much is an ice cream sundae?"

"Fifty cents," replied the waitress.

The young boy pulled a handful of coins from his pocket and started counting them out. This took a while, since he had only started to work with money the previous week.

After a while, he lifted his head and stared at the waitress. "How much is a dish of plain ice cream?" he asked in a squeaky voice.

By now, other patrons had entered the coffee shop and were patiently waiting for the girl in the white apron to take their orders. She became irritated and told the boy, "Thirty-five cents," in a rather harsh tone.

Counting the coins again, the boy finally said, "I will have the plain ice cream, thank you so much, Miss."

The waitress brought the ice cream and the bill a few minutes later and left the boy to enjoy the dish.

The boy finished his ice cream, savouring every moment of the delightful occasion, then he stood up, paid the cashier and silently left the coffee shop.

When the waitress came back to clear the table, she stood there with a lump in her throat.

Beside the empty ice cream plate, was a small heap of coins, totalling fifteen cents – her tip.

Do you see what I mean?

There are just so many things to be grateful for, but we never stop to think about them.

After seeing the picture of the gleaming chocolate sauce dripping off the soft serve, the boy with fifty cents in his pocket really wanted the ice cream sundae. Nonetheless, he was so grateful for the person serving him, that he saw it fit to "downgrade" to the plain ice cream in order to show his appreciation for her hard work.

Remember this: you can never, ever be thankful enough. Gratitude has no ceiling. It can't be boxed in.

Don't be afraid to express your feelings of thankfulness. Write down things you are grateful for and reflect on them before you go to bed. Do not keep your gratitude to yourself. Thank people when they are kind to you or serve you (even if they get paid for the service they provide).

Showing gratefulness will also condition your mind to stop worrying about all those potential problems that are giving you headaches – like the professor's heavy glass of water – and focus your thoughts on the much more important positive aspects.

The real troubles in your life are apt to be things that never crossed your worried mind; the kind that blindside you at 4 p.m. on an idle Sunday.

Deal with these troubles as and when they occur instead of trying to anticipate them. Use the time you previously spent on worrying about "potential" obstacles to be grateful and to believe in yourself.

Be thankful to your mysterious donor and for the 1,440 minutes she deposits into your time bank account every day at 00:00 a.m. Use this time wisely and keep on telling yourself, "I should be grateful for every minute I get to live on this planet."

* * *

There is a saying that if you have forgotten the language of gratitude, you will never be on speaking terms with happiness. There also might be a lot more truth in that than meets the eye. Several studies have shown unhappiness to be inversely associated with gratitude. It seems that the more grateful a person is, the less miserable they are.

A clinical psychologist, at Eastern Washington University in the United States, found that clinically depressed people showed significantly lower gratitude (nearly fifty per cent less) than his controls – non-depressed people.

In another study on gratitude, conducted by a professor at the University of California, random participants were given one of three tasks to write in a journal each week.

The first group had to describe five things they were grateful for that had occurred in the previous week.

The second group had to record daily troubles and difficulties that annoyed them during the previous week.

The third group (the neutral group) was asked to list any five events or circumstances that influenced their lives in the week, but they were not instructed to focus on the either the positive or the negative.

Ten weeks later, participants in the gratitude group felt more optimistic about their lives in general and were a full twenty-five per cent happier than the group recording the negative events. They also reported fewer health complaints and were exercising more than the negative group.

Even in the neutral group, people who had written about gratitude were diagnosed as more cheerful than those who had recorded events that displeased them.

You can do this too.

When you experience something to be thankful for during the day, make a voice note to yourself on your mobile phone, or write it down. Then listen to it or read it aloud in the evening before you go to bed.

You will be surprised by how much better you will sleep after hearing things like, "I am so very grateful for the opportunity to eat healthy food every day," or, "I am incredibly thankful for the rain that fell this morning," or "Thanks to all my friends, I made it through a difficult afternoon and came out on top."

The positivity of gratitude will aid you in believing in yourself more.

I have found that when I take time to appreciate the customers my business has landed (and the income they provide) my mindset goes into a mode of giving back to society.

When customers make payments on invoices, I try to give back to society; usually to a less fortunate organisation in the same industry.

For example, if a customer in the candle business makes a payment to my company, I might take on an initiative of, for instance, providing some solar lighting for another struggling company for a year.

Remember: the more grateful you are, the more you will start to enjoy everything you do and life will just feel so much better.

People appreciate the special words "thank you" so much and I really think that we could use them more in today's world.

Be grateful for your family. Although you may have your ups and downs with them, they will *always* be there for you.

A practice my wife and I have introduced into our lives, is to stop for a moment and name five things that we love about each other or that we are grateful for.

For example, with my wife, five things about her that I am grateful and love about her are:

“I am grateful for her humour”, “I thank her for believing in me”, "I am thankful that she is always caring and worries about me", "I love how she lights up the room with her smile when she walks in" and “I am grateful that she is a good mother to our kids”.

It helps us to appreciate each other more and to see the bigger picture in our marriage and our family. We both adore our two beautiful kids and we are incredibly grateful for having them in our lives.

* * *

There is a concept called the missing tile syndrome.

If you look at a roof or a floor and there is a tile missing, you keep on staring at that missing tile, instead of realising that the rest of the roof or the floor is perfectly fine.

In life we also sometimes tend to focus on what is *missing*, instead of being grateful for what we *have*.

We often worry so much about bad things happening to us, that we never zoom out and see the beauty of the roof or the floor; the beauty of our lives.

Appreciate everything you have, because many others have less than you. Instead of wondering whether the glass is half full or half empty, be grateful that there is water in the glass at all.

All right, then. You have prepared for the journey to greatness by adopting the habit of strengthening your self-belief for twenty minutes every morning, and by accepting that more gratitude will increase this self-belief.

Let us put the plan in motion, shall we?

CHAPTER 4

Take action

Y

ou are now ready to divide your twenty early morning minutes into two segments. Use the first ten minutes to affirm your self-belief and the next ten minutes to plan.

I cannot stress enough the importance of good planning. I know it sounds obvious, but there are so many people who get this part wrong.

A proper plan means to well and truly understand what you want to achieve. A plan is not a dream, it is something you *intend* to do rather than something you *want* to do; a vision rather than a fantasy.

Let's say you have believed in your ability to save money to such an extent that you are now in a position to build your dream house. You decide to design the house yourself and afterwards give it over to the architects and building contractors to dot the i's and cross the t's. It is January and you want to engage with the architects within six months.

Here is an example of a poorly constructed plan:

- Complete outside design – 28 Feb
- Complete inside design – 31 May
- Review with Jane – 2 June
- Minor adjustments – 15 June
- Meet with architects – 30 June

This plan tells me nothing. It's purely a timeline and that should not be the intention of a plan.

Good planning involves focus and understanding. Set your milestones according to what you really want the outcome to be. Otherwise, you might achieve your goal but still feel unsatisfied afterwards. Make life exciting!

Challenge yourself with detail. Ask yourself questions by visualising the end result. You can do this as a mind map or with the aid of some other visual toolsets. After this, you can take the vision and create your detailed plan.

I would consider something like this a proper plan for designing your new house:

- Floorplan draft – 15 Feb

North facing bedrooms (5)
En-suite bathrooms (2: main + guest)
Other bathrooms (2: only showers, no baths)
Kitchen size? (discuss with Jane)
Entertainment area – upstairs
Lounge with fireplace – downstairs

- Inside finishes – 28 Mar

Bottom floor (tiles? laminated wood?)
Top floor (carpets: colour? texture?)
Cupboards – bedroom (wood? colour?)

Cupboards – kitchen (wood? colour?)
Lights (downlights? voltage?)

- Discuss light effects in movie room with Jeff next door

Paint (silky, pearl white – compare pricing)
Ceilings + double volume lounge (calculate)
Bathroom accessories

- Attend the Bathroom Bizarre exhibition on 24 March
- Get quotes for all accessories

▪ Outside finishes – 03 May

Walls – paint + insulation + thickness
Roof (work with different angles)
Pool area – built-in day beds

- Pool tiles + pool lights
- Pool dining area + deck, cover & patio
- Jacuzzi

Glass doors, folding wooden doors
Lawn area and tennis court

▪ Surroundings – 01 Jun

Driveway and fountains
Palisade (wood vs. steel)
Front gate & security
Garages

▪ Final review with Jane – 2 Jun
▪ Minor adjustments – 15 June

Remember copies of original design

▪ Meet with architects – 30 June

This is called a visual plan and could be used for achieving any goal. Note that the plan contains enough detail to envisage the dream but not too much to make everything complicated. The important point is to break down your milestones into smaller, manageable ones.

If you have started up a new business, for instance, and you want twenty customers by the end of the year, break it down and set targets for one customer per month for the first four months and then increase the goal to two customers a month for the remainder of the year.

The same goes for relationship improvements, fitness goals, spiritual goals, financial stability, learning a new language, social goals, or any other dream you are chasing.

Sometimes, sequencing can be important. Perhaps not in the house design example but in certain other goals it might be essential to determine the sequence of events. You cannot drive a car until you have switched on the ignition, for example. You cannot decorate a cake until you've baked it.

Plan smart, plan visual and plan in small building blocks.

It is also essential to have a clear vision and a final destination in mind. You can't reach the destination on your roadmap when you don't know what that destination is.

* * *

Once you have determined your destination and defined your visual roadmap, the next question is: "How on earth am I going to execute this lot?"

Here is where the tricky part comes in. No matter how strong you believe in yourself, don't for one moment think the execution of your plan is going to be easy. Yes, your self-belief will significantly increase your success rate, but it will still be hard work.

Nonetheless, now that you have identified an opportunity to improve your life, you need to grab it with both hands, no matter how hard it's going to be to make it a reality. Seize every opportunity whenever it comes your way.

Before you can do this, however, you have to overcome your fears first.

We all have them: fears that seem to hold us back.

But here's the surprise: Sometimes it can be more scary if we don't do what we want to do, because then we will never really see our full potential. So, face your fears by using your immense new power, self-belief.

Never underestimate this power. It will help you to confront all your fears and begin to take action. With total devotion and concentration, anything can be accomplished.

Prior to taking action, ask yourself this question: "What would my actions be if I had no fear whatsoever?"

You'll be surprised by how quickly that will change your thought process from discouragement to motivation.

According to a popular online dictionary, the definition of the word **action** is: *the fact or process of doing something, typically to achieve an aim.*

The key in initialising action is taking the first step.

Once you have done that, the rest will fall in place like a jigsaw puzzle. Following your dreams always seem to become easier after you've taken the first step. I know that from years of experience.

If, for some or other reason, you fail in achieving one of the smaller milestones you have defined, do not stress. Remember: there is a big difference between the word *fail* and the word *failure*. When you fail, it does not make you a failure. Not at all.

Have you ever watched a bird building a nest? It's fascinating, really. In the beginning, it looks like the most cumbersome and hardest task in the world for the poor little bird. Yet, one morning, you wake up and voila! There is the nest! The only problem is, a day or two later, the nest falls to the ground. It might have been a cat, it might have been pure gravity, who knows? Then the building of a new nest commences. No trying to repair the old nest, no trying to recover material from the wreckage. No sir – the little bird starts from scratch!

That shows us the power of persistence.

Have faith in your ability to execute your plan but if you fail, start again and use one of the other important weapons in your armoury to assist you: hope.

Hope, together with believing in yourself, creates a strong combination of expectation and a desire to succeed. It will keep you going through the tough times.

Focus your efforts on what truly matters. You need to know what counts and what doesn't. Change only what you are able to change and let go of the rest.

Have courage.

The Formula One racing car driver, Niki Lauda, was leading the world championship rankings when his car veered off the track and slammed into a barrier before bursting into flames at the German Grand Prix in Nürburg. He was trapped inside the burning vehicle for almost a minute and by the time he was pulled from the wreckage by other drivers who had stopped to help, his face was burnt beyond recognition.

Six weeks after receiving last rites in his hospital bed, Lauda surprised the world of motorsport by taking part in the Italian Grand Prix in Monza. He didn't do this to prove a point – he did it because he had the *courage* to do so. Still in bandages, after having suffered first- to third-degree burns all over his face and hands, and having inhaled toxic fumes that damaged his lungs, he finished fourth. To this day, it remains one of the sport's most memorable acts of courage and defiance.

So, be courageous in pursuing your dreams – even if it requires you to step out of your comfort zone – and know your strengths. Take control and become the pilot of your vessel of dreams. Believe in the magic inside you; we all have it. The secret is to find it and expose it.

Time is your friend. You can achieve much more in one hour than you think, believe me.

Do not forget to celebrate.

Whenever you have reached one of your milestones, congratulate yourself. Whether it is just a pat on your own back, or a dinner with a loved one, or a glass of good red wine while watching the sun go down, celebrate and smile. That overall feeling of happiness reduces your heart rate, reduces the effect of pain and stress, and calms the body overall, making you more efficient and extra productive in achieving the next milestone or goal.

Follow a healthy diet. The brain doesn't function very well on fast foods and sugary drinks.

Research which foods you need to eat to cover a balanced diet. For example: allicin in garlic and antioxidants in grapefruit to clean the liver, sodium in cauliflower and blueberries for the kidneys, lutein in egg yolk to strengthen the eyes, healthy fats such as avocado, nuts and seeds for the pancreas, prunes for the heart, and omega-3 fatty acids in salmon, tuna and sardines for the brain.

Taking action is about grabbing the bull by the horns and you will need all the strength you can get.

And don't forget the sunscreen…

Wait, what? you will think. *What does sunscreen have to do with believing in myself and reaching for my dreams*?

Absolutely nothing, is the answer. It's only a metaphor.

It means protect yourself against harmful external factors. Put checks and balances in place and cover yourself against these factors. If your goal is to live in a non-English speaking country, learn their language and study their culture before you leave. If your goal is to save x amount of money in five years, make provision for inflation, interest rate changes and the consumer price index. However, if reaching your objective involves a lot of time outside during summer, I would still recommend…

…the sunscreen.

* * *

Listen to the positive voices in your head. Some people call this a gut feel or an intuition and you will recognise it instantly. It's a loud voice or a nagging thought urging you to greatness, and it keeps on telling you that you will be successful no matter what.

In pursuing this inner voice, don't think out of the box, think out of the world.

Take a moment to consider the following three cases and then ask yourself whether any of them would have materialised without thinking out of this world:

One: Airbnb is the world's biggest accommodation provider, yet it owns no property.

Two: Uber is the primary global transport provider, yet it does not own a single vehicle.

Three: Amazon is the largest retail outlet worldwide, yet it does not carry any inventory.

These are companies that control the interface between the consumer and the provider of the goods or services. They carry none of the costs but take a cut from the millions of consumers that buy from them.

This just proves something the Spanish artist Pablo Picasso once said: "Everything you can imagine is real."

While you are imagining, be efficient.

There is a common misconception that efficiency is about getting things done faster and faster. This is not true. Let me give you an example.

You and your friends go out one weekend for a canoeing experience on the river. Arriving at the raft rental place, you select one of the sleek and modern-looking canoes while your friends all take the old traditional ones.

Everybody is excited and, after a quick lesson about paddling from an instructor, everybody is in one of the rental canoes on the water.

When you start to paddle, you want to show your friends a thing or two, so you go as fast as you can. The dilemma is that you don't have the skills to keep the boat stable, so you end up spending more energy trying to be stable than actually paddling. Therefore, you actually go slower than the more traditional, stable canoes of your friends.

The lesson is never sacrifice stability for speed. In life, we sometimes take on challenges and then unequally distribute commitment, instead of honestly assessing what we can really commit to. The result is regression and poorer performance.

The same goes for your goals.

Don't try to rush a dream that isn't conducive to rushing. Sure, some things can be achieved faster than others, but this is not always the case.

Carefully analyse your goals and decide on a productive way to chase them. Sometimes the journey provides more satisfaction than the actual destination.

Now, let us talk about the dreaded d-word again: *doubt.*

I am not going to avoid the brutal reality of doubt in this book. To contend with doubt is critical while travelling on your path to success. We all have those miserable days when we doubt ourselves and our goals feel somewhat unreachable and far away.

While taking action and executing your plans, this doubt will attempt to hinder your progress. Doubt is often the reason people give up on their dreams.

I have touched on the subject of hope before.

Hope is the antibiotic to fight doubt; it will quickly counter the doubts in your mind.

Think of hope as your fallback plan. Hope feels like a cool water fountain in the mountains or like a soft cotton blanket on your skin. Hope smells like a freshly baked muffin and tastes like pure honey straight from a honeycomb.

So, whenever you're in doubt, always cling to that glimmer of hope that will keep you going.

You can even go further and transform the hope in your mind into belief and then turn it into action. Urge yourself to do better and make sure you understand your challenges.

Whenever you are faced with more questions than answers, just believe in your ability to overcome these difficulties. More often than not, they are easier to solve than meets the eye. In the end, it is not about *how* you solve your problems but *whether* you solve them.

A lot of people get stuck in a rut and think: *Oh well, this is my life and it's never going to change.*

But, if you think about it biologically, we actually change every single day. For instance, liver cell regeneration constantly takes place inside your body. One can argue that on a microbiological level we are never always the same person, we keep on changing. Remember: the only thing that doesn't change is change itself.

Just as your body has an automatic ability to reinvent itself, your mind has the ability to reinvent your life.

Did you know that it takes only three weeks to form a habit? So, if you want to lose weight, for instance, and you go to the gym consistently for three weeks, it will become part of your life and serve an even greater purpose than only losing weight. Break your milestones down into days to form this habit. After day one, you only have twenty days left. That is how you achieve your goals and follow your dreams.

Never give up on your dreams.

Speak your success as a present fact, not a future plan.

Instead of saying: "I hope to do that one day," rather say, "I am strategising how to do that right now."

Instead of thinking: *I will be happy when I am in a different place in my life*, rather think, *I am completely capable of being happy right here and right now, nothing is holding me back.*

* * *

There is a game called *I have never*.

For those of you not familiar with it, it's a drinking game usually played by students and it is quite easy to play.

Here's how: I will start a round by saying something like, "I *have never* slept in an alley."

Then you evaluate the statement by turning it into a question: "Have *I* ever slept in an alley?" If the answer is yes, you have to take a drink and I continue with my next statement. If the answer is no, I must drink up and it's your turn to make a statement.

The reason why I am mentioning a silly game such as *I have never* here, is because I have created a variation on the words that works extremely well when you are doubting yourself:

*I **willnever*** instead of *I have never*.

Go stand in front of a mirror and take a look at yourself – not at the reflection of your image, but at your soul.

Now take a deep breath and say: "I **will never** give up on my dreams. I **will never** allow any doubts to stop me from achieving my goals."

Lift your chin and pull back your shoulders. Can you feel the positive blood rushing through your veins? Good.

CHAPTER 5

Confront negative influences

The easiest dark force to find on earth is someone who says you can't do something. I like to call them the "naysayers". Don't believe these sceptics, they don't know you as well as you know yourself.

If you listen to them, they will destroy your self-belief.

If you get angry with them or hate them, they will destroy your hope. Besides, hate and anger have never achieved anything good ever since human existence began.

Send those people love and stay positive.

When I came back from the United States to start my own business – after I had already proved all the naysayers wrong by making a success out of my career in New York City – I was amazed by the amount of negative thoughts from people back in Australia. "It will never work, Adrian," many naysayers said to me. "Are you out of your mind?" others asked. "How can you start your own business without a client base?" And some of them even used the sarcastic cliché: "Let me know how that works out for you, mate."

But I did start my own business and it was up and running – and successful – within a matter of six weeks.

I used the Yellow Pages and began to cold-call hundreds of numbers in order to find new customers. I was refused and rejected many times but, like our bird building its nest, I never gave up. I persisted, I believed in myself, and that glimmer of hope kept me going. Whenever I felt miserable and doubted myself, I repeated the words in my mind: "I will *never* give up on my dream".

Believe in yourself, not in the naysayers. They don't know what they are talking about because, subconsciously, it is in their nature to be negative.

This we have learned from the story about the frog and the scorpion. For those of you who don't know the tale, here is just a brief summary.

There is a scorpion that wants to cross a river but, as we all know, scorpions can't swim. So, the scorpion goes to the frog and asks for a ride. The frog says, "If I give you a ride on my back, you will go on and sting me."

The scorpion replies, "It would not be in my interest to sting you since, as I'll be on your back we both would drown." The frog thinks about this logic for a while and finally agrees to take the scorpion to the other side.

The frog loads the scorpion on his back and braves the waters. Halfway across the river, the frog feels a burning spear in his side and realises that the scorpion has stung him after all. As they both sink beneath the water the frog cries out, "Why did you sting me, Mr Scorpion, for now we both will drown?"

The scorpion replies, “I can’t help it, it is in my nature.”

Some of the people in our society have become scorpions over time. It’s in their nature to be negative and it’s in their nature to shoot you down if you want to chase your dreams. These are the same people that always introduce problems instead of solutions into conversations.

A large portion of the human race has become a scared and confused species.

Can we change this for the better?

Of course we can.

How?

Through positive thoughts and positive actions.

Is it easy?

No.

Is it possible?

Yes.

That is the main difference between successful and unsuccessful people in the world: the winners focus on the *possible* rather than on the *easy*. The easy will look after itself, the possible must be put in motion by YOU.

Remember the compliments you receive, forget the insults; become more virtuous than the naysayers. That is by far the best way to confront negative influences.

These naysayers are going to call you crazy when you explain your goals and dreams to them. They are going to call you insane even to believe you can achieve your ambitions.

Do not listen. Take a deep breath and believe in yourself. You must never allow yourself to become a victim of other people's negative statements. You are not pursuing your dreams for their sake, you are doing it for yourself.

Another way of dealing with the naysayers is to protect your dreams at all cost.

Imagine you are trying to plant a row of trees in your garden. Now imagine you have two extremely vindictive neighbours on each side of your property.

You start to dig the holes but the malicious neighbour on your left keeps on filling the holes with concrete.

You decide not to be discouraged and dig new holes to plant your trees. But the next morning, you find that the trees had been ripped out by the spiteful neighbour on your right.

After taking my advice and breathing deeply, you realise that this is a lost cause. No matter how much self-belief you have, you will not complete this task because two negative people are, unfortunately, stronger than one positive mind.

Outsmart them. Do things differently.

I've always been passionate about doing things differently. It is something I have done all my life.

Protect your precious project. Fence off the area where you are going to plant the trees, hire a guard, plant the trees late at night while your neighbours are asleep, buy a Rottweiler to safeguard your property. Do anything in your power to protect your tree project.

You can do the same while pursuing your dreams and goals. Safeguard them from the naysayers. Tell other people very little about your plans (except for your support structure, of course, but more about that in chapter ten).

This might sound like a bit of a paradox to some people but, while protecting your dreams and not revealing too much, stay true to yourself. If someone asks you outright about your goals, answer them honestly. Otherwise, they will most likely see through you and you will soon be perceived as a fraud by the outside world.

But try to refrain from responding to people when you are attacked verbally.

Always remember that you cannot hold grudges against the naysayers – they are scorpions; it's in their nature.

When I told you about the scorpion and the frog earlier, another frog story crossed my mind.

A group of frogs were hopping through the woods when two of them fell into a deep, dark pit. When the other frogs saw how deep the pit was, they told the two trapped frogs that there was no hope left for them. However, the two frogs ignored the comments from their comrades and proceeded to attempt to jump out of the pit.

Despite their best efforts, the group of frogs at the top of the pit were still saying that they should just give up as they would never make it out.

Eventually, after thirty minutes of jumping, one of the frogs listened to what the others were saying and he gave up. The other frog continued to jump as hard as he could. Once again, the group of frogs at the top of the pit yelled at him to stop the pain and to just forget about getting out.

He ignored them, and jumped even harder until he finally made it out of the pit. When he got out, the other frogs said, "Did you not hear us shouting? We told you to stay down there, buddy."

The frog who had rescued himself then explained to the others that he was deaf, and that he thought they were encouraging him the entire time.

Beautiful, isn't it?

Never give up. Always believe in yourself and always embrace positivity. Never listen to the naysayers – who are subconsciously trying to inject their doubts into your mind – and always have hope.

That mindset, together with proper planning and a well-defined destination, will allow you to succeed in reaching your goals, no matter how big the obstacles in your way.

When confronted by a naysayer, think to yourself whether this person will actually have the guts to chase the dreams that you are chasing now. Is he or she actively involved in life or just sitting on the sideline, judging? If the answer is the latter, then this person cannot add any value to your life.

Shift your mindset and tell yourself that the naysayers are wasting your time and energy. Rather spend this valuable energy to achieve your goals. Or you can redirect the conversation away from yourself, in a positive way by saying something like, "So, tell me about your goals in life. What are your dreams and aspirations?"

* * *

When Novak Djokovic turned thirty years old, he reached one of the biggest slumps in his career. Although he was still ranked the number two men's tennis player in the world, he was struggling to win matches and the naysayers predicted that the end of his career was in sight.

Djokovic ignored these naysayers and worked hard, but by the end of the year he had dropped to his lowest ranking in ten years: twelfth. It was almost looking like the naysayers could have been right this time.

But then Novak Djokovic thought about something he had said to a journalist almost three years earlier:

"So what if you failed? Nobody succeeded without learning to fall first. And by that, I don't mean an easy fall. So go forward no matter what. Fall hard on your nose, and then stand up and keep going forward and fall again and then bounce back again. And then you will win. Keep going and keep standing strong on your feet."

This inspired him to prove those naysayers wrong and he went on to win two Grand Slam titles the following year: Wimbledon and the US Open; pushing his total number of Grand Slam titles up to a staggering fourteen.

He overcame adversity by believing in himself and by persevering.

He didn't allow the negative statements to drag him down.

I do the same, but not without the help of true friends.

My lifelong friend, Hamish, whom I met in year four at school, has always supported me in stopping the naysayers from dragging me down.

On his first day at our school I told him, "Hey, you're the new boy, right?" He was new and self-conscious so he started crying. Later we became the best of friends and we still are today, more than thirty years later.

Although we've only lived in the same city for six years, we've kept our friendship going through all these years.

It just proves that you don't have to be in constant contact with your friends to make the relationship work. Whenever Hamish and I speak or meet face to face we just naturally pick up from where we've left off the previous time.

Make sure you have someone who is always there for you and always supports you in whatever you do.

When I was working in New York, there was a homeless man that would write quotes on the sidewalk. On my way into work one day he wrote, "You are your best investment." Ever since then I've acknowledged the drive within myself and found motivation to succeed in whatever I set my sights on.

Another homeless man in New York was handing out stickers that said, "Mean People Suck." These incidents have resonated with me ever since and encouraged me to work hard and spread kindness.

Here is a sentence about naysayers I want you to write down and then strike through with a black permanent marker.

What if they are right, and I am wrong?

~~What if they are right and I am wrong?~~

That's it, you are never going to ask yourself that question again. Not today and not in a million years.

CHAPTER 6

Have a vision

Visualisation can create inspiration.

We live in a world littered with visual inspirations. We have state-of-the-art virtual reality devices, holographic display units and high-tech 3D printers creating models of houses, modern art and bio-molecular reproductions.

But, before we start to visualise, let us recap on what has been discussed so far:

Take a deep breath – spend twenty minutes each morning to affirm your self-belief and to plan the roadmap to achieve your goals and dreams.

Be grateful – there will always be dozens of things to be thankful for while embarking on your journey.

Take action – plan in small building blocks and execute productively by being persistent and meticulous.

Confront negative influences – refrain from listening to the naysayers; believe in yourself and stay positive.

All right then, back to visualisation.

Have you ever seen a lame advertisement on a billboard and then told your friends about it afterwards?

"Hey, guys, have you seen that stupid new steakhouse billboard at the mall entrance?"

Just that sentence means that the marketing gurus for the steakhouse have succeeded in their goal. The fact that the ad came across as dumb in your mind is not what is of significance. The fact that you *remember* it is important. That is what the original intention behind the billboard was; imprint the idea into people's brains.

The reason why you remember it is because it is big, in your face and "out there". That is the purpose of visualisation.

Do the following experiment.

Ask one of your friends to drive you to town while you are blindfolded. Take your cell phone with you and record all your observations along the way. What the sky looks like, how many traffic lights you pass, what other cars are on the road and which buildings and traffic signs you pass…

Pretty impossible while blindfolded, right?

That's not half of your problems. Keep the blindfold on and – without any assistance from your friend – buy a red sweater, a green pair of flip-flops and a black scribble pad with blue lines on the inside pages.

Can you now see the importance of visualisation? Can you see how difficult it is to take action without vision?

Take the blindfold off and be grateful for your eyesight. This is just one of the many privileges we take for granted from day to day.

Since you have been blessed with the sight of vision, why not make use of it in achieving your dreams?

Type it out in colour (preferably with some pictures), print it and blow it up into a vision board. Then place it in a prominent place to allow you to remind yourself of your ideal life, your goals or your wishes.

It could be your dream home, the ideal partner, a perfect job or a lean and fit body.

Create your vision board and place it somewhere where you will see it every day.

Also, it doesn't have to be only one vision board. You can make three or four; one for your fridge in the kitchen, one for outside in the garden – for your twenty minute morning sessions – and a smaller one for your car's dashboard.

You can go even further and create a progress chart for tracking headway on your milestones. Position this progress chart below your vision board and make it a living plan.

Using our house design example from earlier, a vision board could look like this:

OUR NEW HOUSE...
LOVING IT!

And a progress chart could look like this:

- Floorplan draft – 15 Feb **60%**

North facing bedrooms **100%**

En-suite bathrooms **50% - guest remains**

Other bathrooms **100%**

Kitchen size **behind schedule: fast track**

Entertainment area – upstairs

Lounge with fireplace – downstairs

- Inside finishes – 28 Mar **15%**

Bottom floor (laminated wood) **30%**

Top floor (carpets: colour? texture?)

Cupboards – bedroom (wood? colour?)

These visual aids will constantly remind you of your goals. In addition to reminding you of your goals, the vision board will motivate you, discipline you, and successfully combat procrastination.

If you miss a milestone's deadline, do not panic. Urge yourself to work harder and to be more productive. Mark these missed deadlines in red on your progress chart and leave them red until you have caught up and are back on track. Once they are done, fix green sticky notes over them and mark them as complete.

Ensure that the progress chart stays as green as possible and ensure that your vision board projects a positive message.

A Japanese scientist who said that human consciousness has an effect on the molecular structure of water. His hypothesis was that water could react to positive thoughts and words and that polluted water could be cleaned through positive visualisation.

He started experimenting by taping paper strips with words like HATE and ANGER on certain bottles of water and then on different bottles he used words like BEAUTIFUL and LOVE. He would look at the bottles and think about the words and the emotions they portrayed as he read them aloud in his laboratory.

Then, after a few days, he froze the bottles of water and afterwards examined the aesthetic properties of the resulting ice crystals with microscopic photography.

His theory was confirmed when he noticed that the ice crystals from the water with the more loving words were more pleasing to the eye than their counterparts with the negative words on them. These "angry" crystals were slightly distorted in nature. He had found a way to change the nature of the water by projecting positive or negative thoughts and visions onto it. Astonishing, but true.

Just like the Japanese scientist changed the nature of water, we can change the nature of our thoughts and actions by using positive messages on our vision boards.

Sometimes it just takes a little shift in perspective to help us to see the word differently or to ignite our imagination.

If you see positivity every day, you will start to act in a positive manner and it will become a habit in your life. Whether you use a Pinterest board, blog, notebook or physical board, put together words and images that represent what you want and how you want to live.

Your vision board should also focus on how you want to feel, not just on the things you want. A vision board creates an emotional connection that inspires and motivates you. The more your board focuses on how you want to feel, the more it will come to life through your emotions.

All right, now that you have a clear picture of what your goals are and know exactly what your dream life looks like, you must become the person who is living that life.

The good thing about this visualisation process is that it has already triggered the right actions in your subconscious.

You have already changed and, although you may not feel like it right away, you will soon realise that you are now acting more positively; that you are making better decisions in life and that you are attracting confident people and positive circumstances.

Another important factor is to make sure you look at your vision board every day before you go to sleep.

The time you spend visualising in the evening, just before you go to bed, is extremely powerful because of your subconscious mind. The thoughts and images that go through your head during the last half an hour before falling asleep are the ones that will replay over and over in your subconscious during your night's rest.

If anything during the day didn't go the way you planned it, re-live it in your thoughts as if it went perfectly fine. That way you create positive energy in your mind, carrying them into your dreams and your subconscious.

* * *

Not having a vision is almost like driving around in a foreign country without a map, a GPS or a mobile phone.

For those of you who have difficulties in creating a vision, here is a trick that always succeeds: Start at the end of your life and then work backwards. Project where you would want your life to be when you are old.

This approach makes it much easier than to ask, "Where would I like to be in five or ten years from now?"

If you start at the end and say, "When I'm old I would want to sit down on my porch and think of my family, the dream house I'm living in, all the places I have travelled to and my successful business or job I have just retired from."

I did this before I came back to Australia all those years ago. When I was working in New York City at such a young age, I enjoyed my job, but sometimes I felt a little empty inside, as if something was missing.

Not knowing where my life was taking me was extremely frustrating.

Then I realised that I was unhappy because I didn't have a vision. This wasn't necessarily a bad thing; my feelings of unhappiness told me to move on and they became a motivator for me to create a vision in life.

At first, I was sad to leave New York but then a friend of mine said, "Adrian, New York is not going anywhere. You can come and visit at any time. Go chase your dreams in Australia. Donna Karan runs *DKNY* in New York and she doesn't even live in the city. She flies around the world to look after her business. If she can do it, so can you."

I guess the moral of the story is: if you want to achieve your ultimate goals and that means leaving places or people behind, do it.

This doesn't require you let to let go of them, it just means that your focus has shifted into another direction. You can go back at any time to visit these people and places, even it takes some time in the beginning.

* * *

No matter how good your vision board has been designed, always understand that the power of achieving success isn't in the images or the words.

It's in you.

You have to work hard to reach your goals and – while overcoming your fear – you *have* to remove yourself from your comfort zone.

I can tell you now, as long as you remain inside your comfort zone, nothing substantial will happen on your journey. It doesn't mean that your life will be bad, but it will be no more than average.

Many of the great achievements in the world, such as the Apollo moon landing, the invention of remote control technology and plasma screens, have been accomplished by having a clear vision, not by chance.

The most important thing about your vision is to act it out. A vision board will never become a reality if you don't take action to make it happen. Take that first step and walk your vision to success.

I have also found that focusing on positive thoughts and visualising them gives you the confidence to express yourself.

Growing up, I felt that I never fitted in at school as I didn't know how to be myself and I cared too much of what others thought about me.

Now that I believe in me, I have learned that I don't care what others think so much anymore and it was one of the hardest lessons I have ever had to learn.

But I did it and it gave me the confidence to chase my dreams.

Here is another little secret about being yourself:

Don't change your personality when you leave your home to go to work or school or university every day. If you treat colleagues and clients the same way you treat your family, they will feel the love and contagious energy radiating from a positive extrovert and a caring friend.

Become that person.

* * *

Be mindful of your vision when it comes to chasing your dreams. Do not allow things to snowball and don't allow the realisation of your dreams to become the only thing in life that will give you happiness.

There is a concept I like to call the *Happiness Syndrome*.

This happens to people who spend their whole life searching for happiness. It never eventuates, because they are always searching for something bigger or better.

For example, you beging with, *I'll be happy when I finish high school.*

Then you start with university and think, *Okay, I'll be happy once I get my degree.*

Then it becomes, *I'll be happy when I get a full-time job.*

Then, *when I get married, when I have kids, when the kids grow up, when the kids finish school.*

You can understand how this can quickly turn into a vicious circle.

Don't become a "dog chasing its tail" otherwise you may *never* be happy.

Stop and focus on being happy already and be grateful for what you have in life.

Instead of saying, "I'll be happy when..." rather say, "Today I am happy because…."

One last thought about having a vision: When you follow a vision and you start to become unhappy, stop immediately.

Listen to your inner thoughts, amend your vision to something that will make you happy and then adjust your vision board accordingly…

All right, let us now see how changing your mindset can positively influence your vision.

CHAPTER 7

Mind your thoughts.

Imagine you could squeeze a ten billion terabyte drive into a computer drive the size of a grain of sand. Fine sand.

Now multiply your ten billion terabyte sand drive by another hundred billion and then combine it all into a compounded hard drive.

Can you comprehend the digital storage capacity?

You will be able to store the information from more than a thousand World Wide Webs! Yet, this storage capacity does not even scratch the surface of the colossal, unlimited storage capacity of your brain.

The brain is arguably the most important organ in the human body. It is indirectly responsible for all our senses – see, hear, smell, feel and taste – as well as the motor neurons that make our muscles move. In addition, the brain is in charge of all decision making and all thought processes.

Take a look at the technology and infrastructure around you: the smartphone in your hand, the laptop on your desk, the microwave oven in your kitchen, the television in your lounge, cars, skyscrapers, electricity, planes, radio waves. All of this only exists because of the human brain.

It is the most powerful instrument in the world.

Your brain will process tragedy, romance, happiness, grief, friendship, pride, gratitude and a hundred other emotions. Your brain rules your life.

Sit down tonight and think about everything you know today that you didn't know yesterday. This might sound like a simple exercise at first glance but it's not, I promise you. You have to recall every single conversation you had, everything you heard on the news, what you read on the internet, new things you saw, textures, tastes, smells, new messages on your email, videos from online streaming sites, phone messages, bumper stickers and billboards.

All of this is automatically added to the brain's hard drive every single day. You can retrieve the information whenever you want to and you never have worry about running out of storage capacity.

Let's say you decide to go for a jog around the block in your neighbourhood. You dress in a t-shirt, shorts and a pair of sneakers, then you walk outside and start jogging. A third of the way into your journey you accidentally fall down, but luckily you don't injure yourself. Arriving back home, you take a large bottle of water out of the fridge and drink half of it.

In completing this task of a ten-minute jog (and falling down once) you have actually performed 28 actions. Of the 28, a whopping 24 were performed by your brain, while only 4 were performed involuntary by your body.

24 voluntary actions performed by the brain:

- Opening the cupboard
- Choosing the t-shirt, shorts and sneakers to wear
- Putting the clothes on
- Walking to the front door
- Unlocking the front door
- Opening and closing the door
- Locking the door again
- Putting one foot in front of the other to start jogging
- Seeing people, dogs and cars in the street
- Smelling the flowers in your neighbour's garden
- Hearing birds and cars and people talking
- Lifting your hand to wave at someone
- Using your voice to say, "Hello there, neighbour."
- Feeling drops of perspiration trickling in your neck
- Pushing yourself up after the fall
- Coming to a halt back at your house
- Unlocking the door
- Opening and closing the door
- Locking the door
- Walking to the kitchen
- Opening the fridge
- Taking out the bottle of water
- Unscrewing the cap
- Tasting the water's texture

4 involuntary actions performed by the body:

- Breathing
- Perspiring

- Falling down
- Swallowing the water

Let us then use this impressive tool called the brain to help us achieve our goals and dreams.

First of all, do not permit your brain to listen to any negative thoughts whatsoever.

Sure, we all have bad days and it is only normal to think negatively sometimes, but you can actively stop this by replacing it with positive thoughts. Remember: what you reap is what you sow.

The biggest problem with negative thoughts is that it allows fear of failure back into our lives.

One of my Australian friends always said that she wanted to be a Hollywood actress, but she couldn't live in the United States because she didn't have a green card.

"Adrian, if I ever win the green card lottery," she told me, "I'm going to move to Los Angeles and I am going to be a successful Hollywood actress."

That was her dream in life and guess what? She entered the green card lottery and she won, against all odds! So, off to America she went in pursuit of her career in acting.

However, the experience in Hollywood was just too overwhelming and, after six months, she gave up and came back to Australia. Because she doubted herself, the fear of not succeeding was forever nagging in the back of her head. She couldn't break through her comfort zone because the fear in her mind was holding her back.

You have to fight this fear by filling your brain's storage capacity with optimism and self-encouragement. The fear will often return, so this is a continuous process on your journey to success. Sometimes you're ahead, sometimes you're behind. The race is long and, in the end, it is only run with yourself and your thoughts.

Be watchful of your thoughts in general.

There is a quote about life progression, originally by Lao Tzu: "Watch your thoughts, they become your words; watch your words, they become your actions; watch your actions, they become your habits; watch your habits, they become your character; watch your character, it becomes your destiny."

Perception drives all of us, which is characterised by the thoughts in our minds. What we target in life, or the way we respond to external factors, is guided by our thoughts. Evidently, the character and content of these thoughts define the way we live our lives.

When I finished school, I didn't know what to do with my life. I decided on advertising but, although there were a number of courses on the topic, there were no bachelor degrees from a university. So, I did an economics degree majoring in marketing and economics. It wasn't as exciting as it sounded and I wanted more practical experience. However, I persisted and laboured through university and then, when I finally achieved my degree, an inner voice told me to move to New York to start my career.

This inner voice was nothing more than a positive and optimistic thought in my brain, reinforced by a book by Susan Jeffers, called *Feel the fear and do it anyway.*

Without worrying too much about the logistics regarding a place to stay or a plane ticket, I began to email various advertising agencies in New York, asking them to employ me. I persisted and I was eventually hired – and made a huge success out of it.

If I hadn't listened to the inner voice (thought) in my brain, I would never have had the courage to go through with my fantastic plan.

Not too long ago, Oprah Winfrey, one of my inspirations in life, made a speech about success. She stated the following: "There is only one goal in life, and that is to fulfil the highest, most truthful expression of yourself as a human being. You want to max out your humanity by using your energy to lift yourself up..."

Then she went on to say, "Whether you call it soul or spirit, or higher self, there is a light inside all of us that illuminates our very human 'beingness', if we let it."

Remember: Your thinking style controls and dictates your life experiences. If you want to use your brain to help you achieve your dreams, you have to stay true to yourself and forever be an opportunist. The secret to opportunities is to identify them and then pounce on them. They are all around you, but not always visible to the naked eye.

There is a story about a man who was drowning in the ocean, praying to God, "Please can you rescue me, Lord?"

After a while, a little boat came by and the skipper threw a rope into the water, saying, "Hey, grab the rope! We're here to save you."

"No, thank you," the man replied. "I'm all right, God is coming to save me."

Another bigger boat came by and also tried to rescue the man. Once again, he declined by saying, "Look, I have prayed and God is going to come to my rescue."

Then a big freight tanker arrived and the captain urged, "Please come on board, otherwise you will drown!"

The man, now too tired to even paddle anymore, said, "I'm perfectly fine, God will be here any second to save me." Shortly afterwards his head was submerged in the water and he drowned.

When he arrived at the gates of heaven, he asked God, incredulously, "Why didn't you answer my prayers and save me when I was drowning?"

God looked him in the eyes and said, "I tried *three* times to rescue you and you turned it down each time."

Sometimes, in life, there are signs and miracles coming our way and we have to try to be open to them. We are often so blindsided, that we don't see these opportunities. Recognise your amazing chances, seize them and take action. You might not have a second chance at them.

Train your mind to look out for these opportunities.

"Happiness can be achieved through training the mind," the Dalai Lama once said.

The next logical question would be: “But how do I train my mind?”

It’s very much like a physical workout, actually.

Just like the muscles in your body, your brain needs exercise to keep it from rusting. And the easiest way to help yourself remember what you observe is repetition.

For example, if you get introduced to someone new and that person says, “Hi, my name is Adam.”

Instead of responding with: “Nice to meet you”, rather reply with: “Nice to meet you, Adam.”

Repeat things you learn by saying them aloud or by thinking about them and echoing them in your mind.

Try to learn something new every now and again. You can keep your brain stimulated by starting a new habit, taking up a new sport or joining an interest group. Learning something new creates new neural pathways in your brain. Repeating actions over and over again, reinforces these newly formed brain pathways.

When people work out in a gym, you don’t see them going at it forever. There are “sets” and “resting phases.”

It is important to rest your brain regularly.

If you want to work hard, you have to learn to relax and allow yourself to recover. These recovery periods may vary in length. A ten-minute power nap or a night’s rest or a weekend away are equally effective.

Focus on relaxation as productively as you focus on your goals. Don't just go away to some place for the weekend – force yourself to quieten down and truly enjoy the time without working for a while.

A day without your mobile phone can do wonders for inner peace and resting the mind.

However, do not binge-rest and lose track of the purpose of brain relaxation. Then you will crave even more time-outs because you will become addicted to it.

You have to find the right equilibrium and give yourself the correct recovery dosage. We are all different in this need. The trigger is that inner voice I talked about earlier. When the inner voice begins to say, "Hey, you need to get back to chasing your dreams," listen to it.

Another vital habit in mind recovery is humour.

Do not take comments from other people too personally, find trivial things to laugh about, and try to make others laugh, without being offensive.

You can give positive thinking and positive tactics a great deal of meaning in your life by repeating them to yourself. Once they get lodged in your head, your brain starts to say, *That was easy*, and mechanically starts thinking about other positive strategies.

Redirect everything that is negative and is not supporting your goals and your dreams.

Redirect them by asking yourself, *What would be the absolute opposite of this negative point*? Then think hard about this resulting positive point. Place emphasis on it and keep on repeating it.

The more you take constructive action, the more your brain becomes trained to realise this is how you do things. You can condition your mind without doing anything other than behaving in a more positive manner.

If you don't read a lot, try to read more.

Studies showed that reading exposes you to new concepts (fiction or non-fiction) and can condition your mind to process these new ideas. In addition, reading significantly improves your vocabulary and increases your language skills and articulation.

Write with your hand.

In today's day and age, we are confined to touch screens, keyboards and other fancy devices.

Although these devices provide effective ways of recording information, you can learn much more efficiently by writing longhand.

This is because your brain's sifting section, the reticular activating system, deals with what you are concentrating on at any given moment. Writing triggers this system and tells your brain that it's time to pay attention.

So, when it comes to exercising your mind, try to write things down. It doesn't mean you have to put your phone away; there are hundreds of apps you can use to write with a stylus pen.

Do the stuff you love.

This might seem obvious, but a lot of people don't get it. One of the best ways to train your mind to be more positive is to make time for something that you absolutely love.

The actual event isn't important. Just make sure you love it. It may be playing card games, cooking up a storm, going to a live concert, camping with friends, or going for a spa treatment. Try to set aside some time during each week that will allow you to enjoy events that give you real happiness.

Trust in the higher version of yourself.

You are more proficient than you think you are. You can improve your life dramatically by positive visualisation and believing in yourself.

Remember: Our thoughts need to be clear enough to define our destiny.

A lot of people understand this concept the wrong way around. They suppose that they think a certain way because of their circumstances, not realising that they have it back to front. It is essentially the power of thought that creates those circumstances in the first place.

Your thinking is you. Taking responsibility for your actions begins by taking responsibility for your thoughts.

Steve Jobs once said, "Those people crazy enough to think they can change the world, usually do."

Trust your intuitions.

You know all the answers, you just need to learn how to ask yourself the right questions.

When you experience an awful day – you know, those days when nothing goes your way; you get a flat tire, you're late for an important appointment, and someone spills coffee all over you – combat this by positive thoughts.

Convince yourself that things will get better.

If you keep on thinking, *I am having such a bad day*, it could carry on into the next day, and then the next, until you get to a point where you live a negative life altogether.

So, trick yourself into positive thinking. Smile, breathe, be grateful, and say, "Today is going to turn out to be an awesome day!" Essential oils may assist you in this regard. I find that aromatherapy of these oils is very helpful to induce relaxation and ease my mind.

When you wake up, create a short one-minute movie in your head about how positive the day is going to pan out. Try to start this movie by exercising physically.

Physical exercise releases endorphins that stimulates your brain and your nervous system. Even if you are not a "gym person", take a walk or a jog and start your day by getting those muscles moving. If you want to start to exercise regularly, try to make use of a trainer or a mentor. They will motivate you to keep going.

After the opening scene of your physical workout, play the rest of the movie in your head during the day.

You are going to achieve everything you have planned for the day and it is going to turn out splendid. For example, your date this evening is going to be perfect and you are going to get home feeling relaxed and peaceful.

This movie is extremely important to your mindset and your positive thoughts. It will get you through those difficult times when nothing seems to work for you.

Your diet is also vital to your thought processes. Sugar, for instance, influences our moods in a great way. If you could limit the amount of sugar in your diet, it would be tremendously beneficial to your mindset.

Do not underestimate the power of music. Your favourite music tracks will always lift your mood and elevate your spirit. Sing with the music, even if you are the world's worst singer, do it. It will soon release the tension in your mind and create a cheerful feeling.

Connect with nature's energy. Make time to go to a park or the beach or the woods. Take off your shoes and feel the earth, it will make you feel alive.

Use your positive thoughts to turn those downward spiralling days into upward spiralling days.

We have all experienced this: as soon as one thing goes right, then another one does, and then yet another one. It quickly becomes a positive chain of events.

Remember: You can't control what is thrown at you, but you can control the way you react to it.

Do yourself a favour and think about these words before you go to bed tonight:

Stay humble. Think positive. Be kind.

CHAPTER 8

Take time to reflect

A while ago, I saw the ten-year challenge thing on social media and thought I'd use that to reflect on my life. My very first thought was: *Wow, where has the time gone*? I looked at a picture of me on my honeymoon in Fiji. Ten years later, I was in Fiji again, but fifteen kilograms lighter thanks to changing my lifestyle.

I have realised that grains, dairy and sugar don't agree with my body, so I eliminated them from my diet. I also realised the importance of physical exercise. I really do believe that exercising does turn back the clock.

Everyone always tells me that they do not have time to exercise but you know what? You simply have to make time for wellness and mental health.

You are your best investment and if you don't put your oxygen mask on first, your world and family around you won't last. Age is just a number, don't let that put limits on what you can achieve physically.

I didn't go cold turkey overnight with my lifestyle – I did it in baby steps and you can too, just believe in yourself.

Adrian and Michelle - 11 years ago

Adrian and Michelle Today

Adrian before and after 10 years apart

Take a moment to reflect on what has happened in your life over the past year.

What did you achieve?

What did you attempt to achieve but fail at?

What did you do that made you or other people around you proud this year?

Taking account of your past accomplishments (and failures) will help you recognise what you need to work on in future.

Don't limit your time to reflect only on study your vision board or your progress chart. Stand back and give yourself a thirty-thousand-foot view of where you are in life. See the bigger picture every now and then. What are you satisfied with and what could be changed for the better?

While evaluating your successes, be honest and establish whether you have impressed yourself. If you cannot establish this by asking yourself questions, ask others.

A young man once walked into a pharmacy and said to the pharmacist, “Can I perhaps pay you five dollars to use your telephone? I don’t have a cell phone and I can’t find a pay phone anywhere.”

The pharmacist agreed and the young man telephoned a certain company to ask about a job as an office clerk.

He was told: “The job has been filled a week ago.”

“Is the clerk you have satisfactory?” he asked.

“Very satisfactory!” was the answer.

The young man hung up with a big smile on his face.

The pharmacist, who had overheard the conversation, was slightly puzzled. “If the job is filled, how come you are so happy?” he inquired.

“Oh, I was just checking up,” replied the young man. “You see, I am the office clerk they employed a week ago.”

That is a perfect example of doing something different to reflect on your achievements.

While reflecting, celebrate your successes and congratulate yourself. If you want to also reward yourself, do it but not by buying tasty treats; you are not a household pet. If you want to buy something, rather buy yourself a new shirt or a necklace or go on an exciting adventure.

Study your failures but don't become fixated with them. The majority of failures can be categorised into two groups: 1. Not working hard enough, 2. Setting your goals too high.

If you have failed because of scenario 1 (not working hard enough), first ask yourself: "Could I have put in a better effort? Could I have spent more time or been more efficient in chasing this target?"

If the answer is yes, simply work harder and smarter next time. If the answer is no, then you are most probably facing scenario 2 (setting your goals too high). Recalibrate your expectations and change your milestone timelines.

Here you have to go back to your progress chart and become an investigator. Scrutinise your timelines and break your goals down into smaller, more manageable milestones. Set more realistic targets.

Whenever you reflect on and measure your achievements, make sure you keep a journal. Write down what you've done right and write down what you've done wrong. Then fix the wrongs and learn from them.

Once you have learned from your mistakes, make some adjustments for better future actions.

We all know Albert Einstein's age-old saying: *The very definition of insanity is doing the same thing over and over again, but expecting different results.*

Learn not only from your mistakes but also from your achievements and successes.

"*Everything* in life is a lesson," Novak Djokovic once said.

* * *

Reflective practices are methods and techniques that help us look back on our experiences and actions in order to engage in a continuous learning process. It enables us to recognise behaviour that shapes our thinking and actions.

Self-reflection is about asking yourself probing questions so that you can develop a better level of understanding your strengths and weaknesses.

During self-reflection you can change how you view yourself and how you feel about certain situations.

It's all about understanding and making sense of what transpired in the past year, quarter, month, week or day. Once you have this awareness, you can develop a new vision, then the goals to achieve that vision, and then smaller milestones to reach those goals.

The biggest mistake people make with self-reflection is that they interrogate themselves from *within* themselves. Unfortunately, that will not provide you with the correct answers. If you want to reflect efficiently, you have to find a way to climb out of your body and do it from the outside.

Let's say you have been entrusted to arrange a high school reunion party for a hundred people. Suddenly you are faced with two problems. One: you simply don't have the time to organise this party. Two: you don't have the experience; you've never arranged a party for more than twenty people. The only thing you have to work with is money – all the partygoers have paid an upfront entrance fee.

So, what do you do? You hire an external contractor to perform the job on your behalf. You engage in a detailed planning session where you explain to the contractor your requirements, the budget and the details of the party.

Afterwards you assess the contractor's success by asking a number of questions. Was the party within budget? Was the venue big enough? Was there enough food and drinks for everyone? Did the decorations meet the standard of your specification? Was the music appropriate?

You are asking these questions because you are assessing *someone else*. With self-reflection you have to do the same.

Ask yourself questions as if you were someone else.

Become an investigative reporter and speak to yourself in the third person: "Adrian, why did you perform that action when two other alternatives were available?"

Proper self-reflection can help you to apply your thoughts and expand your ideas, grow your conceptual and analytical skills, as well as becoming more aware of your actions.

Here is a mental exercise you can perform while taking the time to reflect:

Write down a noteworthy event that recently happened to you. Then answer some of these questions: Why was this event significant to me? What underlying issues surfaced because of this event? How will the occurrence of the event influence my future behaviour?

Other things to think about while reflecting are your past efforts, time management, achievements, overcoming fear of failure (getting out of your comfort zone), changes in your behaviour, and whether you are enjoying life.

To reflect is to interrogate your inner self. Keep on asking yourself questions. Have I done anything lately that is worth remembering? Have I made someone smile today? To what degree have I actually controlled the course of my life? Which is worse: failing or never trying?

Another method of self-reflection is *free associations.*

The practice of free associations is a technique used in psychoanalysis. In the free association process, you have to transform all your thoughts into words without any filters, even if those thoughts are somewhat loose, incoherent, inappropriate, or even irrelevant. Psychoanalysts encourage you to mention anything that comes to mind.

It's an advanced technique you can use for self-reflection. You go to a quiet place, take a pen and a piece of paper (or your journal), and start writing down whatever comes to mind. Do not use any filters at all. After that, you try to analyse your thoughts one by one. In the process, never forget that the list of free associations you produced is somehow related to your present situation. You just need to try to find out how and why.

The story of the curious puppy is all about self-reflection.

There was an abandoned house with broken windows and no doors in a forest somewhere. One day, the puppy found this house. He noticed that the house had no people living in it, but he was afraid to go too close. However, this puppy was a bit of a curious one. The next day he returned and went a little closer to the house, but still did not go in.

All of a sudden there was a hailstorm and the puppy had no choice but to run for the cover of the house.

Inside, it was completely deserted. He barked in the lounge on the ground floor but nobody answered him. He then trotted up the stairs and, to his surprise, came across a large room with hundreds of puppies just like him! They all appeared to be waiting there for him.

The curious puppy was so happy. The other dogs were very friendly and that gave him the confidence to raise his little paw and greet them. Everyone greeted him back and when he gave a friendly bark, the others did the same.

What a nice place! he thought. *I'll come back to this house whenever I can!*

The days went by and then another puppy came to the woods. This one was different though; he was much more fearful than the first one.

He went through the same process as the previous puppy. When he saw the house, he did not want to go near it. But then there came a massive hurricane and he also had no choice; he had to go inside the house. Similar to the first puppy, he barked in the lounge and no one answered. He could see the stairs but he was too afraid to go up.

After a while he got quite cold and decided that it might be warmer upstairs. He cautiously walked up the stairs and arrived in the room where there were hundreds of other dogs, that looked just like him. He instantly prepared to attack, and the other dogs did the same. He barked aggressively and so did the others. Realising that he was heavily outnumbered, the second puppy ran downstairs and left the house as fast as he could.

What a terrible place! he thought. He left so quickly that he failed to see the sign on the floor that read: "Welcome to the House of Mirrors". Neither the first puppy nor the second one had grasped that all they had seen were reflections of their own images.

The story of the curious puppy shows us something that we often overlook. What we see in others is in many cases a reflection of ourselves. The story makes us think if it's perhaps time for some positive self-reflection.

In order to achieve this positive reflection, there is a tool that can assist you. It's called a self-awareness worksheet.

This worksheet contains concepts to help you reflect on your aptitude, potential, values, and perceptions.

A typical self-awareness worksheet will contain several sections, each of which has a set of questions and prompts for you to contemplate and reflect on.

Here is an example:

<u>ADRIAN's SELF-AWARENESS WORKSHEET</u>

Aptitude

What are my greatest skills in life?

Which one of these skills gives me the biggest sense of pride or satisfaction?

How can I use these skills in achieving my dreams?

Values

Make a list of ten principles that are really important to you.

Which is the most important one?

How can these values assist me in reaching my goals?

Perception

How is the "public me" different from the "private me"?

What do I want other people to think about me?

Is it more essential to be liked by others or to be myself? Why is that important to me?

Achievements

What are the three accomplishments I am proudest of in my life to date?

What do I hope to achieve in the next six months?

If I could achieve only one more thing before I died, what would it be?

Finish the phrase

I am at my absolute best when . . .

I struggle to operate properly when . . .

I am relaxed and cheerful when . . .

I feel pressure and tension when . . .

Being myself is sometimes difficult because . . .

I am comfortable in being myself when . . .

The five words I would like to live by are . . .

I feel most energised when . . .

I feel tired and distraught when . . .

I am going to make my life all about . . .

General

Make a list of everything that really inspires you. Whether they are books, movies, quotes, people, art, technology, occurrences in nature, or spiritual matters.

What do I love most about life?

Which is the one skill I need to teach myself to help me live a more fulfilling life?

* * *

That is just one example of a self-awareness worksheet. There are many out there, so choose one that suits your personality and fits the goals you are trying to achieve. You can also get creative and combine some of them or generate your own.

Remember: someone with a good understanding and execution of self-reflection is someone who will be able to manage their impulses. Reflection and self-awareness are your soundboards; your sanity checks.

You have to understand that life is a continuous learning process and that you need to make adjustments all the time. This is the only way to support your self-belief effectively. If you don't reflect on your actions, you will soon be caught up in chasing empty dreams.

Don't make the mistake of living your life like the grass-eating lion.

A pregnant lioness goes out to hunt and finds a herd of deer. While attacking them, a deer's horns fatally injures her and she dies giving birth to a little male cub.

The cub has nowhere to go and the herd of deer adopts him.

Growing up, the little lion imitates everything the deer do, including having a diet of grass and leaves. However, because his body isn't receptive to this food, he soon begins to become sick all the time.

He is unhappy, malnourished and weak.

Years later, another lioness attacks the herd of deer and notices the weak lion. "What is wrong with you?" she asks. "Why are you eating grass and why on earth are you grunting like a deer?"

"Because I am a deer," answers the weak lion, barely able to stand on his feet.

"No you're not," replies the lioness. "You're a lion."

She takes him to a nearby pond and makes him look at his reflection in the water.

"See that," she says. "You are a lion. You need to eat meat to survive, not grass and leaves."

The weak lion, astonished, thinks to himself, *No wonder I am feeling so frail and depressed all the time. I have been living another animal's life!*

He opens his mouth and makes a tiny roar for the very first time ever. His heart swells with pride.

"Come," says the lioness, "follow me into the woods and I will teach you how to become a real lion."

Look at yourself from that perspective when you reflect again and make sure you are not perhaps living someone else's life by mistake.

Honest self-reflection opens your mind to reprogramming, change, success and freedom...

* * *

If you do not control your life, then others will.

And in order to take charge of your own life, you have to start to write down and reflect on your actions as well as all the events around you.

I began to save for a deposit for a home when I was thirteen years old, only because I could foresee that as something I would need later in life.

But you cannot foresee your future until you've reflected on your past. I believe we can project our thoughts forward and backward in time. In doing that, we can change the outcome of certain events.

Ponder this: You walk out of your front door and think to yourself, *Let me check if I have the door keys in my pocket.* Perhaps – because the door has a self-locking mechanism – your mind had jumped forward a few moments (when you forgot your keys and locked yourself out) and then returned, warning you to prevent the sticky situation.

That is called involuntary reflection.

Nevertheless, you also have to make time for voluntary reflection, otherwise you will fall around in a life without purpose and without meaning.

Taking time to reflect will improve the best investment you have ever made in life: YOU.

CHAPTER 9

Give back

People often say that they cannot give anything back to society because they do not have millions in their bank accounts like Oprah Winfrey.

Well, before the *Oprah Winfrey Charitable Foundation* came to light, Oprah had another charity organisation called *Oprah's Angel Network*. She didn't use her own money for this – she asked the viewers of her television show to donate their change, as well as their time and effort.

This charity fund raised millions of dollars, which was given away in the form of scholarships, and mustered fifteen thousand volunteers to build homes for the *Habitat for Humanity* project. Many more millions of dollars went to relief efforts in the aftermath of hurricanes Katrina and Rita. The network also helped to build sixty schools in thirteen countries and to provide books and uniforms.

Something Oprah said about giving back is very important to keep in the back of your mind: "The greatest gift you can give someone is to see and hear them. You have no idea of the power of noticing another human being and what it feels like when someone knows they have been seen. It is the greatest gift you can give."

Be generous with everything in life. Be generous with your generosity. You don't have to give money, but rather your time, efforts and care. If you have a special talent, use it to help others in some or other way. If you have unused facilities, lend them to others who need them. If you have the authority to effect change for the better, then apply it. If you have influence, use it.

I have been actively involved in a charity organisation called *The Shepherd Centre* in Australia.

One Australian child is identified with significant hearing loss every day. *The Shepherd Centre's* vision is that every child with hearing loss can achieve their full potential in the world through listening, spoken and written language, and social skills.

Early detection and support is crucial in supporting a child with hearing loss so that they can attend mainstream schools with their hearing buddies.

The Shepherd Centre has incredible success rates, with 95% of its graduates attending a mainstream school and the speech skills of these kids are often superior to their peers, despite only receiving 30% funding from the government.

A cause close to my heart, with one of my kids attending *The Shepherd Centre*, I have experienced first-hand its amazing work, which could not be achieved without the thousands of helping hands supporting it.

You could also be one of those helping hands at a charity organisation in your own country.

So, try to give back where you can and, in doing so, remember the following:

There are three types of people when it comes to giving back to society.

The bottom third is a group of lazy, apathetic people who have forgotten the basic principles of survival and need everyone else to help them make a living.

The next third is the group of self-sufficient humans. They make a living for themselves, but that's it. They don't contribute to the world, except for themselves.

The top third is the group of people that changes the world for the better. They look after themselves but also lend a hand to others. They donate their time, money, effort and expertise to add value wherever they can. They attend public forums, assist charity organisations, look after the less fortunate and plant trees.

I urge you to be part of this top third group of people.

There is an anonymous quote that says: *Strive to be first: first to nod, first to smile, first to compliment, first to give and first to forgive.*

* * *

Academy Award winning actor, Matt Damon, is an example of a true humanitarian. He is making a serious impact off-screen by working towards ending global poverty.

As a young boy, Matt travelled to countries like Mexico and Guatemala, which inspired his passion for environmental and social change.

His humanitarian efforts first began when he became aware about the poor water quality and sanitation in Africa. Soon after that realisation, he started a non-profit organisation to help people access clean water and better sanitation.

Receiving the Environmental Media Association award on three occasions, this charity organisation has made a positive impact on more than seventeen million people by the beginning of 2019, providing them with clean water they'd never had access to previously. By finding effective water solutions, Matt Damon is indirectly also fighting sickness, poverty and crime.

Instead of only giving money for the cause, he is actively involved in his organisation's projects, travelling all over the world to bring clean water and better sanitation to disadvantaged communities.

In addition, he has developed a clever water credit program, which helps the poor to play an active role in finding infrastructure solutions.

Matt is also a co-founder of the charity organisation, *The Sentry*, which supports and inspires global human rights. This organisation is working to assist with issues around the globe that are not getting the deserved consideration from various world leaders. Even with his busy schedule in acting, screenwriting and producing, Matt Damon still makes time to help our world with his philanthropy.

What can you do to make a difference here on earth?

* * *

I have been so honoured to work with such amazing clients over the past sixteen years and I know it sounds clichéd, but I am truly lucky that I get to do what I love every day and work with my believe dream team here in the office. I have always believed in giving back to those less fortunate than myself.

Through the power of PR, I have learnt that I can make a difference by highlighting worthy causes that need attention to the world. After helping a young lady with cancer to raise funds for a charity close to her heart, being able to support a Fijian village that I had the pleasure of visiting on a recent trip and highlighting the good work of The Shepherd Centre – helping young kids with hearing loss develop spoken language, my aim is to leave this world a better place than when I found it.

Adrian at MaloMalo School

Adrian with Batiri School Principal Mr Dinesh and Kids

At Believe Advertising & PR we pride ourselves on choosing charitable projects each month to support in honour of the publicity work that we have implemented for our clients.

* * *

People sometimes say that they understand that it is *morally* the right thing to do to give back, but that doesn't make sense *practically*."If I give my money and possessions away, how will I be able to survive myself?"

Let me prove the contrary:

Imagine you get lost in the mountains during a hiking trip.

You are on your own with only a sleeping bag, a tent, your cell phone and some food supplies. There is no telephone network coverage and you cannot call anyone or download a compass app. After trying to find your way back to the main path for almost two days, your food and water supplies are critically low and your phone's battery has died. Just as you think you are going to die here in the mountains, you come to a fenced-off grass patch with three things inside: a fresh water fountain, a chicken and a walnut tree.

You can't believe your luck. The chicken lays an egg every day and every morning there are between eight and ten walnuts on the ground that fell from the tree.

Surviving on the handful of walnuts and a raw egg a day, you still hope that someone will come to your rescue. However, after five days, the chicken dies and you have to do with only the walnuts. Eight to ten walnuts a day are not enough to keep you going, so you start to pluck more walnuts from the tree. By day twelve, all the walnuts are depleted and you only have fresh water left.

By the end of day twenty-one – two days before a rescue helicopter arrives – you die of starvation.

Now let us rewind twenty-one days.

Think about what you could have done better and where things went wrong. That's right, you didn't give back. You were selfish to eat all the walnuts on the ground. You see, before you arrived, that was the chicken's only source of food. You took it away and that's why the chicken died.

Had you shared the walnuts on the ground with the chicken, it would have lived much longer than five days and you would have made it all the way to day twenty-three, when the helicopter would have rescued you.

The moral of the story? Always share and always give back.

The Dalai Lama said: "Be kind whenever possible. It is always possible."

* * *

I firmly believe in the law of attraction and the law of energy. When you give back, whether it's your time, effort or money, you will receive in return ten times more, because that's the way the energy of life works.

So, if you are sitting at home thinking, *I have no money and no job prospects, what should I do?* go out there and start giving back to society.

While you are doing that you might, for instance, be referred to a job or attract money in the process. But the secret is to make sure you give back for the right reasons. Don't do it because you are looking for the law of attraction or energy to affect you. Do it from the goodness of your heart and those other benefits will come in time.

Giving back and making a difference in someone else's life will cause you to feel good and will improve your overall positive mindset, effectively making a difference in your own life as well. I guess what I'm trying to say is that being generous can be a kind of healing therapy.

Allow me to take you back to chapter three of this book (Be grateful) where I discussed the influence of gratitude. In reality, the action of giving back is actually a form of gratitude, which in turn elevates your energy levels and makes you believe in yourself more.

By doing this, you are saying thank you for the fact that you are more privileged than others.

Make sure your giving back is contagious. For example, if someone pays you money for services rendered and you decide to give half of that to a charity organisation, tell that person what you're doing.

That person might just start to do the same and also pay it forward to someone else in need.

* * *

I will never forget something that happened once between a complete stranger and myself. It was the holiday season at the end of the year and I was in a grocery store. There was a lady behind me at the checkout who had a really ill child. I gave her a gift card that she could use on groceries.

I didn't know this woman and I did not want to feel pity for her because of her sick child, but I imagined that she hadn't had an easy life up to that point.

She was so grateful and, to me, doing something for a stranger was one of the most terrific feelings I've ever had. I could feel the energy between two people who have never seen each other before.

If you don't have the financial ability to give back, do it through random acts of kindness.

There are many ways in which you can help others. Start with your inner circle – family, friends, office, school – and then work your way outwards from there.

Whether you are organising a yard sale for charity or visiting an old-age home over a weekend to cheer up the elderly, just go out there, volunteer and give back some of your energy and time to the community.

A quote by the great humanitarian, Nelson Mandela, says: "In Africa there is a concept known as *Ubuntu,* the profound sense that we are human only through the humanity of others; that if we are to accomplish anything in this world, it will in equal measure be due to the work and achievement of others."

You will often find that giving back will teach you some new skills and broaden your knowledge. For example, if you volunteer to assist at a hospital or a medical centre for two hours every Saturday morning, you might learn a lot about the medical profession you've never known before. Likewise, if you volunteer to help build houses for homeless people, you might learn some interesting things about the construction industry.

Begin to recycle, pick up rubbish, donate blood, create bird-feeders, volunteer at an animal shelter, re-connect with an old friend, donate your old clothes to charity, cook a meal for a family in need, hug people more often, adopt a flowerbed, become a mentor, join a community centre, throw down a charity challenge on social media.

There are just so many ways to give back.

Start with the smallest gesture and then grow into the habit of lending a helping hand. Philanthropy will enrich your life and provide your local community (and eventually the whole world) with a better future.

* * *

A fifty-five-year-old homeless man by the name of Billy Harris had once lived on a street corner in Kansas City, Missouri.

On a cold winter's day in February, when he was holding out a paper cup to collect spare change from passers-by, Sarah Darling walked past and dropped some change in his cup.

What she didn't know at the time, was that she had also accidentally dropped her engagement ring in the cup. The ring was slightly too big because her hands were freezing.

Billy took the ring to a nearby jewellery shop and it was valuated at $4000. Standing there in the jewellery shop, looking out the window, Billy (to whom $4000 was an absolute fortune) could not find it in his heart to sell the generous lady's ring. He thanked the jeweller for the valuation, then carefully placed the precious ring in his pocket and returned to his street corner.

Keeping the engagement ring in his pocket, he waited (and hoped) for the nice lady to return. Times were tough on the street, but in his mind's eye he could see how happy she was going to be when she got her ring back.

A number of days later, Sarah Darling followed the route past his street corner again and stopped once more to put some change into Billy's cup.

He stood up, took off his hat and produced the ring from his pocket. "I believe this is yours, ma'am," he said in a humble voice, holding out the ring. "You dropped it in my cup by accident some time ago."

Sarah was almost in tears, not only because of finding her beloved engagement ring again, but because this kind-hearted man – who had basically nothing to live on – had kept it safe for her all this time.

To thank Billy Harris for his brutal honesty and abundant integrity, she and her fiancé created a crowdfunding page that afternoon to raise $1000 for him.

But the members of the local community who read about the story during the following weeks and months, went above and beyond, raising a staggering $190,000 to help "Homeless Harris" get back on his feet.

The money helped him to buy a car and make a down payment on a small house in Kansas City.

The media attention drawn by the story also assisted Billy Harris to reunite with his family, who hadn't seen him in more than sixteen years.

This shows us how the law of energy will return things tenfold (or much more in Billy's case!) when you show kindness and give back to society.

Remember: Taking only five minutes of your time to assist somebody who is struggling, or to motivate someone in need of support, is a form of giving back.

It is never too late to start giving.

CHAPTER 10

Find Support

M

ake sure to surround yourself with positive allies during your journey to success. Start spending more time with people who are supportive, loyal, ambitious and creative.

You cannot rely only on your life partner for this support. He or she may not be the best person to aid you in achieving your goals. Emotionally, yes, but when it comes to expertise, seek out a mentor with the right knowledge. Don't get me wrong, you need support from your family, but on a passionate level rather than on a professional level.

For example, if you want to learn how to water ski and your partner is a snow skiing expert, their advice will not work.

Although the two sports may appear to be the same, they are completely different sports. In the one your arms must be straight, in the other your arms are bent. In the one your feet are moving all the time, while in the other your feet need to be still. In one you lean backwards and in the other one you lean forward.

Similarly, you cannot ask an interior designer to give you legal advice.

Find mentors from different aspects of life who are willing to support you in reaching your goals. If the goal is to lose weight, seek out dieticians and gym instructors. If the goal is to make more money, look for stock brokers, financial advisors and entrepreneurs. If it's to improve your interpersonal relationships, find people like life coaches and psychologists specialising in interpersonal therapy.

You don't want to reinvent the wheel. Some people have been doing certain things their whole life. Learn from the experience of these mentors and allow them to help you.

Make it a win-win situation wherever you can. Let's say you seek out the advice from a yoga trainer to improve your flexibility. You happen to be an expert in graphic design. After your first yoga class, the instructor gives you an invoice with a terrible logo featuring a stickman holding a flimsy yoga mat above his head. The instructor proudly announces that he had designed the logo himself, but admits that he is not very good at it.

Instead of staying quiet, tell the yoga instructor that you will teach him some graphic design techniques and recommend software programs he can use for this purpose.

This then evolves into a mutual mentorship, where both parties benefit from each other's expertise. In addition, the interdependence will cause both parties to feel gratitude towards each other.

Mutual arrangements have been around for thousands of years and have always been working.

Long before the agricultural revolution, and before dogs were domesticated, people used to live and hunt in small bands of twenty to a hundred heads.

At first, these packs of people only used dogs to hunt but, as the two species evolved, they started "communicating" with each other and a mutual agreement began to form.

The humans realised that if they fed the dogs, the dogs would protect them from wild beasts and other enemies. In turn, the dogs figured out that the better they protected their owners, the more food and care they would receive.

So, while you find your mentor in the appropriate life skill, don't be afraid to reveal your own strengths and skills. It could become the perfect mutual relationship.

Support from your loyal mentors will take you a long way towards achieving your goals.

Notice that I mentioned *mentors* (plural) and not mentor. This is important in a case of multi-faceted goals. Many people – who haven't really believed in themselves before – think that they are only going to tackle one goal at a time.

This will change with strong self-belief.

The moment you start chasing one dream, another one appears on the horizon, or another opportunity presents itself. Before you know it, you have three life dreams and six goals supporting them. This is inevitable where people believe in themselves since they are positive, more efficient and have a general lust for life.

You will more likely than not end up with multiple mentors. Where possible, introduce members in this group of people to each other. You never know when one might say, "Oh, by the way, Adrian helped me increase my sales through his publicity services." Then another mentor in the group might say, "That is good to know, since I have a friend in the fashion business who needs some good publicity."

I'm sure you can see where I am going with this.

It goes without saying that the naysayers can never be part of this group of mentors. They will set you up for failure and therefore do not deserve a place at your round table.

Find people you can actually rely on.

If you want to fly like an eagle, don't hang around with the turkeys. People with a negative mindset will drag you down to their level. You must either attempt to make them more positive or stay out of their way. You have the choice to decide who you want to spend time with and who not. Your time is precious. Use it wisely.

Once you start hanging out with people who are unhappy with their lives, you aren't going to receive any support if you try to break out and do your own thing. The other truth is that you will eventually *become* who you spend the most time with. So, choose who that is very cautiously.

Can you support walls properly without a foundation? No.

Can you support a roof without walls or pillars? No.

Your self-belief is your foundation, but you need a support structure to help build this foundation. Your vision board becomes your walls, but you need a support structure to keep them strong. And, ultimately, your actions transform into your roof, the apex of your vision, but you need support against wind and rain (naysayers and obstacles).

* * *

Although I have said before that your life partner cannot be your mentor, that is not always the case.

If you want to design your dream house and your wife or husband is an architect, by all means, let them be your mentor. However, it won't hurt to get a third-party opinion. Sometimes life partners live in a bit of a bubble and need a soundboard to check on their reality.

When the best-selling author, Stephen King, started to write his first novel, *Carrie*, it nearly never saw the light of day, so to speak.

Stephen was a janitor at a high school at the time and decided to write a chilling story about a high school girl with a telekinesis ability.

When he reached page three, he walked into a proverbial brick wall because he had to describe the emotions of teenage girls, a topic about which he had no knowledge.

He crumpled up the pages, threw them in a dustbin in the corner and went to bed.

The next morning, he awoke to find his wife, Tabitha King, sitting at the kitchen table, reading the pages in awe.

“Why did you throw this away?” she said, incredulously. “It’s absolutely brilliant!”

“Well, Tabby” Stephen replied with a sigh, “I don’t know anything about teenage girls.”

“Don’t be silly,” she told him. “I’ll help you with that part, but you have to finish the story! I’m too curious, I want to know how it ends.”

Carrie was published a year or two later and became a best-selling novel within months. By the beginning of 2019, Stephen King had written more than seventy books, with over three-hundred million copies sold.

This is a good example of mutual cooperation. Stephen and Tabitha King are both writers and their shared mentorships support and complement each other.

I am so grateful for my wife, Michelle, who also compliments me in so many ways, not just through work. When working together, she looks after the social media side of things for clients, while I tackle the publicity work but working on separate projects, we ultimately come together and I love this about us. Outside of work, Michelle really does keep me balanced. She helps me realise not to sweat the small stuff and always manages to put things into perspective for me and I am forever grateful that she has come into my life.

* * *

Good mentors will help you with setting goals, as well as assessing whether they are achievable and when. They will also assist in prioritising goals and encourage you to work harder and smarter.

Setbacks and challenges are much easier to face when you have support from a mentor. And, don't forget, it's someone to celebrate with!

Think of this group of mentors as your *success network.*

Now let us add people with other support capabilities to this success network.

First, find a sidekick.

This represents your emotional support when things get hard. Though usually your life partner, it doesn't have to be. It can be a brother, a sister, a friend, or even just a colleague trying to achieve the same goals as yours.

You also need to add a connector.

This is someone who will support you by introducing you to the right people, places, tools and opportunities.

It is a person who has a strong presence and influence in society, with connections in the right places. Someone who will open doors for you.

A father and son, out for an evening walk, came to a place where a big stone was blocking their path.

The little boy tried to lift the stone, but it was far too heavy for him. He finally gave up and shook his head.

His father, who had studied him while he struggled, asked, "Have you used all your strength?"

The boy placed his hands on his hips and confidently replied, "Yes, I have."

The father then said, "No, my son, you have not used all your strength. You haven't asked me to help you out."

That is the sidekick.

The same boy walked with his uncle on another night and they came to a fallen tree, obstructing the path.

After trying to remove it by himself first, the boy said, "Uncle, will you please help me lift this tree?"

His uncle assisted him but they were still not able to move the tree. After a few minutes, the uncle stood up, wiped sweat from his forehead with the back of his hand and said, "Don't worry. I know a farmer with a horsecar not too far from here."

That is the connector.

* * *

You have now created your success network with mentors, sidekicks and connectors. Think about how you can increase the time you spend with them.

Apply the rules you have learnt so far to the people in your success network. Do not take their support for granted, be grateful for them and give back where you can.

Don't be afraid to ask questions.

Mentors, connectors and even sidekicks love questions. Questions help them understand you and your goals better.

Asking questions will also assist in your self-reflection.

Your support structure does not have to stop at your success network; we all need support from anybody close to us.

There is a common misconception that support groups are only for people with problems. This is not true. A support group will strengthen and enhance your vision or your dream in life, as well as motivate you to achieve them.

When the astronaut, Neil Armstrong, became the first human to walk on the moon, he did not do it alone. Back in Houston, there were thousands of engineers, scientists, analysts and flight experts supporting him. And, more importantly, he had the company of fellow astronauts, Edwin Aldrin and Michael Collins, supporting him in the command module during the journey.

The human species isn't designed to operate in isolation from other people.

A smile is support. A hug is support. A few kind words, a handshake, a nod of encouragement, a wink of appreciation, a high-five and a hand on the shoulder are all forms of support that we sometimes take for granted. It's in our nature to want to have people around us, otherwise we become lonely.

Alone is one thing, lonely is something different.

Alone is what you sometimes ask for, or even ache for. We all need some alone time. But *lonely* isn't something we ask for, it's something brought on by unfortunate events. Nobody wants to be lonely. It's a terrible mood depressant and it makes you want to give up on your goals.

There is a film about a man who is stranded on a deserted island after a plane crash, called *Cast Away*.

The main character explores the island and finds that it is uninhabited. He needs to survive and starts to open the *FedEx* packages the cargo plane was carrying.

One of the items he finds in a package is a white volleyball.

After accidentally cutting his hand, the man uses his blood to draw a happy face on the volleyball. He names the face "Wilson" and chats to little Wilson to take away his loneliness during the rest of the film.

In the end, the company of Wilson helps him to survive until a rescue team arrives a few weeks later.

No, we are not made to be lonely. Not at all.

We need people around us and by this I don't mean virtual people like on social media. I'm referring to *real* people. Social media is often a smokescreen. People may seem happy and smiling, but you never know what goes on inside them behind the scenes.

This can have an effect on your mindset. Make some time for a social media detox. Put your phone down and engage with someone in real life.

Make sure you surround yourself with *real* loyal friends and *real* support, instead of just social media contacts. Have real conversations, face to face. Then your support group will become strong enough to help you and guide you through those tough times.

Just like you reflect on your visions and your goals, you have to take time to reflect on your relationships with the people in your success network.

These relationships matter more than you think. Broken relationships will not only have a damaging effect on reaching your goals, but also on your health and personal happiness.

Test the relationships with your mentors, connectors and your sidekick, by performing the following exercise.

Draw a circle in the middle of a page (or screen) and write ME inside. Then write the names of the people in your success network around the circle.

Now, connect these people's names to the circle by using one of four visual connectors: a thick line for unbreakable, a thinner line for strong, a dashed line for weak, and a zigzag line for broken.

You should now have a picture that looks something like this:

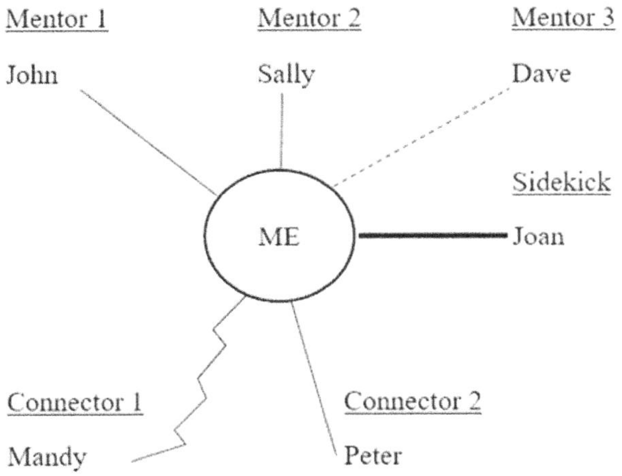

Study your picture and reflect on all the relationships. Pay more attention to the dashed lines (weak connections) and the zigzag lines (broken connections).

Why are they like that?

What can you do to fix them?

Keep in mind that sometimes the problem lies on the other side of the fence. In our example, the relationship with Mandy is broken because the person in the middle said something reckless that hurt her.

That person can apologise, talk about the issue and fix the relationship.

The relationship with Dave, on the other hand, is weak for some reason the person in the middle hasn't figured out yet. Dave just became "cold" somewhere along the line; nobody knows why.

Here – where the potential fix is not in your hands – you need to investigate. Find out why they are not committed to your cause. Find out what holds them back.

While building your support team or success network, you also have to learn to accept the boundaries and prospective of each relationship.

Having said that, make sure that your relationship map never contains more zigzag lines or dashed lines than solid lines.

That indicates only one thing: your team has lost its mojo. Act before your network becomes dysfunctional.

First prize would be to fix the broken lines, but if you are unable to do that, replace some of your support people with better or more suitable matches to your personality.

Very important: your sidekick should always have a thick line (unbreakable relationship).

Again, never stop asking questions. The moment you ask a question, you will liberate the people in your support structure to understand you better and thereby enabling them to provide you with more sound advice.

* * *

Once you believe in yourself and set out on your journey, it will be very much like a ship riding over waves.

Sometimes the waves will be big and other times they will be smaller. The important part is to keep riding and overcome your obstacles.

Along your way, you might lose some people around you and that's okay; if they were truly supportive they would have stayed on your ship.

You will know who those toxic people are.

The ones who are constantly weighing you down, causing your ship to sail slower and slower. They are the brakes that you don't need in your life.

Let them go and move forward.

There is an anonymous quote that says:

You will be too much for some people.
Those aren't your people.

Other people will soon come along and remember: people come into your life at a certain time for a reason.

Losing people along the way might cause you to sometimes feel a little lonely on your journey.

Embrace this and use it to reflect on your dreams. Turn those moments around and use them to empower yourself. Think about how far you've come and how much closer you are to achieving your goals than before the people slowing you down had left.

Don't be afraid to approach life coaches.

I have a business coach by the name of Dale Beaumont who does wonders for me.

Some time ago, he invited me to one of his business workshops and I enrolled in the course. I soon realised how much knowledge he had and how much I could learn from his guidance.

I also have another friend, Kerrie Erwin, who happens to be a celebrity psychic.

I believe everyone has an energy field (consisting of mind body and spirit) around them that has to be managed. Someone like a life coach can help you with that. Instead of being sceptical, rather be open-minded and try to get help from these kind of people.

Kerrie is amazing in that way; she constantly helps me to clear this energy field and reinvent myself.

So, now you understand why loyal support is so critical on your journey to success, and why you need to keep on measuring the relationships in your support network.

CHAPTER 11

Believe!

Every minute of every day is a new opportunity for you to turn your life around.

Believe that you deserve the best life ever. Believe that you can make a difference in the world every single day.

Unfortunately, we never know when our time on earth will be up. We also don't know when someone close to us is not going to be around anymore.

So, make the best of your life and treat every day as if it is the last one you are living.

Many of us have been made aware of the law of attraction by different books, quotes and speeches.

The dilemma is that the law of attraction will not work if you do not believe in yourself.

The one cannot exist without the other. You simply have to have self-belief if you want the law of attraction to affect you in some or other positive way.

Statistically speaking, only eight per cent of people go through with their plans to chase their dreams.

This eight per cent consists of some of the world's most successful and inspirational human beings.

What happens to the other ninety-two per cent then?

It is my opinion that about half of them don't have any dreams at all, while the other half have dreams but do not follow them because they don't believe in themselves. They are too scared to get out of their comfort zones and the fear of failure haunts them every day.

The terms fear and self-belief are mutually exclusive. If you have one, you cannot have the other.

If you stop being afraid, your self-belief will automatically return. If you believe in yourself, your fears will vanish. Don't allow anybody to tell you otherwise – it is what it is.

"Which one do I tackle first?" you might ask. "Dismissing fear or gaining self-belief?"

Evaluate your personality first.

If you are an extrovert by nature, believe in your confidence and your fears will go away.

If you have the strong and quiet personality of an introvert, fight the fear of failure with all your might and your self-belief will eventually manifest itself.

"How do I combat the fear of failure?" the introverts will immediately ask.

As I have said before, ask yourself what you would have done in life if you weren't afraid of anything at all.

Then just do it. Don't think, don't rationalise, just do it.

Never underestimate the power of believing in yourself.

You need to become an addict to self-belief.

* * *

There is one concept that is extremely underrated in our thought processes, and that is the phrase "moving forward".

No matter what the situation, moving forward is always a better route than looking over your shoulder. When a failure occurs, people who do not believe in themselves often get stuck into a mindset of: *What have I done wrong*?

This question can consume a lot of your valuable time, without actually producing any significant results. Instead, rather ask yourself, *What can I do better in future*? That will imprint a positive mindset in your thoughts and will result in the all-important action of "moving forward".

Besides, a positive mindset will make you feel good and cause you to solve most problems more efficiently.

Do the following two exercises (one bad and one good):

First write down the sentence, "Today I have done the following wrong:"

Then add five sentences below that about things you could have done better during the day.

Study your list, let the information sink in and then assess your emotional state. You are most likely going to feel stressful, unhappy and slightly depressed.

Throw away the piece of paper or erase the words from your tablet/phone/computer.

Now write down the following sentence, "Tomorrow, I am going to do better by:"

Then complete the sentence by adding five phrases.

This second exercise are going to make you feel free, happy and determined. It will entrench positivity in your mind and increase your self-belief in general.

You will have a lot more control over your life once you believe in yourself unconditionally. There is only one kind of self-belief and that is the unconditional kind. There can't be any doubt in your mind. If you stick a picture to your fridge with a fridge magnet, you do not spend the whole day worrying about whether the magnet is going to hold, you trust it. Self-belief works in the same way: trust your ability to believe and never doubt yourself.

While you believe in yourself, also believe in your dreams.

Make peace with the fact that, in many cases, one dream can only be achieved by achieving a secondary dream first.

For example, you want to own a beautiful home by the sea, but your financial position does not allow it. In this case, you first have to chase another dream to make more money: get an increase, start a new job, start a second job - anything that will help you generate more income to eventually achieve your initial dream of acquiring your new house.

Something else to think about at this point is time.

I have touched briefly on the subject in chapters two (time is a gift) and three (use your time wisely).

Time is different for everyone. This goes for the time we get to live on earth, but also for the way we experience time.

For instance, astronauts out in space will experience sixteen sunrises and sunsets during one of our twenty-four hour days on earth.

The same can be said about the way we perceive time in our different lives. If you are having a great day, time goes by pretty fast, but when it feels like the world is against you, a day could seem like an eternity.

Whichever way, always make the most of your time and seize every minute to reach for your dreams.

* * *

The world of medicine has evolved in such a way that there is now a pill for just about anything.

Do you want to lower your cholesterol levels? Take a pill. Do you want to counter stress? Take a pill. Do you want to stabilise your sugar levels? Here is your pill.

Yet, there is still no medication to increase self-belief. This has to come from *within* yourself. Only you can achieve it.

Also remember that believing in yourself is a learning process. It is something you can easily teach yourself by following a few principles:

Focus your attention on solutions instead of on problems. The first step in this habit, is to stop complaining about all the things that appear to be making your life difficult. Accept your current situation and then plan on how to improve this situation by positive thinking.

Visualise the outcome of your day, week, month or year with heightened emotion. See in your mind's eye how happy you are going to be in celebrating your successes.

Stop comparing yourself to other people. *You* are the one on the journey to your *own* destiny. The other people (call them passengers if you like) are only spectators.

Try to engage in activities that you are good at and enjoy. In certain cases these activities will align with chasing your goals, in other cases not. Both will improve your self-belief because it reminds you of your talents and your skills.

Don't take constructive criticism personally. Constructive criticism does not come from naysayers, it comes from people who want to help you improve yourself. Turn this positive critique around and use it to make enhancements and positive adjustments in your life.

Always value yourself, and take pride in yourself, no matter what you are busy doing. People who are proud of themselves have self-respect and self-confidence, which will quickly grow into self-belief.

Embrace the unknown. This will help you to overcome your fears. Do something brave every now and again, and start to spend more time with people who are adventurous and spontaneous in nature.

Don't be a follower, be a leader. Sure, not all of us are born leaders, but here I'm talking about taking initiative. This can be achieved simply by your choice of words.

Instead of saying "I think we should..." rather say, "I know from experience..."

Instead of saying, "We should consider..." rather say, "The correct way to handle this is..."

Instead of saying "Why don't we?" rather say, "Allow me to show you the way."

Be assertive and become a leader on a social level. Self-belief and being an initiator is not something you inherit, it is a conscious decision. Tell yourself that you are just as worthy as any other person to take the lead and show the world how things are done.

* * *

A man once visited an elephant sanctuary, and he noticed that none of the elephants were in cages or held by chains.

The only thing that prevented them from escaping was a thin piece of rope tied to one of their legs. As the man was studying the elephants, he was astonished to see that they didn't use their immense strength to break the ropes and escape the camp. They didn't even try.

Curious about this spectacle, he asked one of the trainers, "Why are these big animals just standing there, without trying to escape into the wild?"

The elephant trainer replied, "When they were still young, we used these ropes to tie them. Because they were much smaller, the ropes were strong enough to hold them back. However, as they grew up, they became conditioned to believe that they could not break out. They kept on believing that the ropes were still strong enough to prevent them from escaping, so now they never try to break free."

I guess the moral of the story is: If you keep on believing that the world is holding you back, you will never succeed.

Rather believe in your abilities to achieve anything you can dream of. Believing that you can make a success of something is the most essential step in actually achieving it.

You can do anything!

You weren't born with a label that said what you can or cannot achieve in life.

* * *

Little Eliana Cohen of Miami, Florida, was about to turn two years old when a specialist SMA doctor gave her parents some incredible good news and some equally incredible bad news.

Being diagnosed with Spinal Muscular Atrophy type two, an extremely rare genetic disease, Eliana was unable to stand or walk around, and would have been like that for the rest of her life on earth.

The doctor told her parents that there was a new miracle drug called *Zolgensma* which would recreate the gene that would allow the child to breathe, eat and sit up on her own.

Unfortunately, there were two problems with *Zolgensma*:

One – it was the most expensive drug in the world (2.2 million US Dollars for the single dose treatment).

Two – the drug had to administered before a child reached the age of two (according to the FDA rules).

Eliana was four days away from her second birthday and the family had no money for the medication. Needless to say, their medical insurance also didn't cover it. However, her parents had so much belief in humanity that they created a crowdfunding platform to be able to raise the cash to cure their daughter.

I heard about Eliana's story on Facebook late one night, so I reached out to my international media contacts to get them to write a news story on Eliana's cause. I also reached out to her parents offering my services for free, telling them that I could help them spread the word internationally through a PR campaign.

When I awoke the next morning, the journalists didn't even need to write a story as the amount needed had already been raised through the power of social media. Eliana's donation webpage had reached the 2.2 million Dollar mark needed to save the child.

Her parents and family were overjoyed and grateful beyond comprehension. Just by believing that they could raise the ridiculous amount of cash in four days, they had received money from people from all over the world to make up the total amount in less than two days.

They defied the odds by using the tremendous power of belief. You can do the same by applying this belief in your own life.

* * *

Let us address the topics of entrepreneurship, jobs, and careers briefly.

If you are an employee, having a strong sense of self-belief will finally help you to achieve those key performance indicators that always seem so unachievable. You will display better efficiency and your superiors will soon acknowledge the value you bring to the business.

If you are a manager or a director, self-belief will earn you more respect from your employees and shareholders. Your decision-making will be enhanced and your managerial skills and inter-personal relationships will improve.

If you are an entrepreneur, believing in yourself will allow you to build, expand and grow your business to searing new heights. Customers love organisations that make them say things like: "These guys know what they are doing" or "This supplier is so successful because the owner is self-confident and closely involved in his firm."

They *want* to give opportunities to companies with self-belief, because those are the suppliers they can trust to deliver quality goods and/or services.

* * *

Something that you will quickly notice is that as soon as you start to believe in yourself, your success network and the rest of your support structure will also begin to believe in you. Respect works in the same way: the more self-respect you have, the more others will respect you.

People who respect themselves and believe in themselves are naturally optimistic and have full faith in their abilities.

We can learn from children with regards to this.

Have you ever watched a three-year-old toddler pull on a tablecloth to retrieve an object on the table?

That kid has the self-belief that he or she can attract the object closer by pulling on the tablecloth. What do we, the adults, do? We reprimand them (because it's dangerous) while we should actually encourage them.

The next time you have the opportunity with such a child, make up a table with soft toys on a tablecloth and tell the toddler to pull to their heart's desire.

Do not allow the world to stop you from pulling on the tablecloth. If you believe you can get things done, get them done, no matter what is required and no matter how unorthodox your methods.

The fear of trying something new, only to be disappointed by an embarrassment or a failure, is sometimes enough to stop us dead in our tracks.

Don't be afraid to fail.

Everything might not always go as planned, but that is how we learn. Life isn't just about winning all the time; it's about gaining knowledge and developing your skills. The more you learn the more you will believe you can do it better next time. All of this takes a bit of time, so be patient and have inner peace.

Acquire the ability to forgive yourself.

If you make a mistake, learn from it, then forgive yourself and get over it. Undertake the task again, this time with more determination and a stronger self-belief.

See your vision for a moment as a super high-tech Lear jet that is going to fly around the world in seven days.

There are five goals to accomplish this vision: five stops to refuel in different countries. You start your trip on the west coast of America and then have stopovers in New York, London, Cairo, Hong Kong and, finally, Sydney. These fuel stops (or goals) can also be seen as time to reflect back on the flight and to plan for the next destination.

The milestones to achieve these goals are diagnostics like altitude, speed, fuel consumption and airflow. Your vision board is a map of the world and your progress chart is the aircraft's instrumentation panel. Your support structure, of course, consists of the pilot, the co-pilot and dozens of air-traffic controllers.

All right, you are all set and ready to go, except for one last important thing: jet fuel.

If you don't have enough fuel, you won't reach your first stopover. If you don't have any fuel at all, the plane will not even be able to take off.

Now think of your self-belief as the jet fuel.

Without any self-belief your vision, the Learjet, will sit in the hangar or on the runway's tarmac forever. A beautiful, sleek, impressive aircraft to look at, but totally useless when it comes to achieving your dream operationally.

Do not allow your vision to become a stationary jet on the ground. Add some self-belief fuel whenever you take time to reflect on your goals.

The biggest benefit of believing in yourself is that it grows self-motivation, which is a critical ingredient in following your vision, reaching all your goals and achieving your day-to-day milestones. Psychological studies have shown that a healthy self-belief is considered to be one of the most significant motivators and positive regulators of behaviour in people's everyday lives.

Oprah Winfrey once said, "You don't become what you want, you become what you believe."

Believe in yourself and you will be amazed by the heights you will be able to achieve.

You can do anything!

Just believe.

CHAPTER 12

Wait, too much information! Where do I start?

B

efore we answer this very essential question, ask yourself the following: "What do I want to achieve in life?"

Have your answer ready?

Good.

Now recap on what you've learned so far in this book with that answer in mind:

Take a deep breath – spend twenty minutes each morning to affirm your self-belief and to plan the roadmap to achieve your goals and dreams.

Be grateful – there will always be dozens of things to be thankful for while embarking on your journey.

Take action – plan in small building blocks and execute productively by being persistent and meticulous.

Confront negative influences – refrain from listening to the naysayers; believe in yourself and stay positive.

Have a vision – create your vision board and your progress chart and monitor them often to notice how well you are achieving your dreams, goals and milestones.

Mind your thoughts – you can't control what is thrown at you, but you can control the way you react to it by applying a positive mindset.

Take time to reflect – use a self-awareness worksheet to measure your emotional well-being and to ponder on your achievements.

Give back – get involved in your community and start helping those less fortunate than you.

Find Support – create your success network by finding mentors, connectors and a side-kick.

Now say to yourself: "I believe in myself and my abilities. Because of this, reaching my goals is going to be an easier task than I initially thought it was going to be."

The first thing that you have to do on your journey to success is to stop caring about what other people think of you. Many of us live our lives trying to please others. This inhibits our dreams and can cause a lot of unhappiness.

Unless it is an act of giving back, make sure your goals are about *you*, or about you *and* someone else. Once you do that, you will feel the freedom wash over you.

The worst thing we can do in life is not be ourselves. You will be much happier being yourself than trying to fit in with other people's lives.

* * *

The environment you live in or work in is a reflection of your life. When you live a crazy life and your mind is scattered with thoughts, and you want to become calm and positive, you have to start the process of decluttering.

Throw out old stuff that you don't need anymore (donate them to charity), rearrange furniture in your house and make sure the environment around you is neat and clean.

You will be amazed at how it lifts a lot from your shoulders, renews your energy, and clears your mind. Your environment becomes like a new blank canvas to work on.

Spice up your clothing with colour, even if is only by wearing a bright red scarf or a canary yellow tie. A lot of people feel like they are leading a dull life because their clothes are dull. Colourful clothing will lift your mood and make you feel alive.

Improve your posture. If you straighten your back, lift your chin and pull back your shoulders, you will feel more confident and be able to breathe more easily. If you slump, your mood will too.

Hug people. I always feel we can do this more. Hugging others will not only make them feel good about themselves, it will influence your mindset to feel relaxed and loved.

People save things they value only for special occasions. For instance, "I am going to wear this watch or these shoes only on a special occasion." Or, "We will use this dining set when our guests from out of town are here next month."

Life in itself is special and everyday should be special to you. Make use of everything you have whenever you can. Sure, save some money, but don't go overboard. For example: If you have a mindset of saving your whole life to travel the world when you retire, you might find that at age sixty-five you have the financial capability to travel but your health does not allow it anymore.

So, if you have a bucket list, start ticking the items off today, rather than next month.

Appreciate the small gifts in life, like fresh air to breathe, cold water to drink, a roof over your head and friends and family to support you. This gratitude will leave a warm feeling of happiness in your heart.

We all have our "winter" times.

When the gloomy season of winter arrives, a lot of people stay in their houses and begin to almost hibernate.

You don't have to do that.

It could be mighty cold outside but the sun could still be shining. Dress in warm clothes and go outside for a walk or a jog. It will do wonders for your spirit.

In life, it is pretty much the same. You could be having a miserable day, but there will always be a sun shining somewhere. It might be your kids, a life partner, friends or a beautiful garden. Be very grateful for these little sunny moments and use them to make yourself feel better, even when you are under pressure.

Remember: The most beautiful diamonds are made under tremendous pressure.

* * *

One of the most underestimated words in the English language is "active".

If you think of the word ambition, for instance, it is just another word on your vision board. But if you add the word action in front of it to become "active ambition", it transforms into a different concept. Now, it becomes a purpose and a state of mind.

To be actively involved in something is so much more than just thinking about it.

On the road to your dreams add the word, active, to the other concepts on your vision board: active dreams, active goals, active milestones, active celebrations.

Become the active master of your life on earth.

Active also goes hand in hand with the word, now. Act now and see the results instantly. Procrastinate and you will make life very difficult for yourself in future. Act now.

When an Australian woman, Lauren Prezioso, saw two boys drowning in the ocean at Coffs Harbour Creek, she only hesitated for a split-second before jumping into the sea to save them.

She was eight months pregnant at the time.

Lauren, a strong swimmer who had some lifeguard training under her belt, told news reporters afterwards that in that split-second she was worried about whether she was going to be able to be buoyant enough to swim properly with her transformed body.

Then her courage and self-belief took over and told her two things: *Your unborn baby is going to be okay,* and, *you can save those boys*.

As the boys' mother (who couldn't swim) was screaming for help, Lauren got into the water and swam with the rip current towards the boys.

Grabbing the two children, one in each arm, she struggled back to shore and as she was about to run out of steam, another man came to the rescue and helped the three of them to safety.

The mother of the boys couldn't thank Lauren enough and explained to her that their family had recently moved to Australia from a landlocked country in Africa and none of them knew how to swim. The boys were just splashing in the shallow water when a wave pulled them in.

"I would do the same again in a heartbeat," she told news reporters proudly. "It was a king tide and those boys were going under."

Lauren believed that she could rescue the children, acted instantly and saved their lives in doing so. This is just another great example of the power of self-belief.

* * *

While chasing after your dreams, banish words like anger, hatred, unlikely, sorrow, tension, fear and insecurity from your vocabulary.

Embrace words like love, success, gratitude, happiness, greatness, relaxation and fulfilment.

If you find yourself angry or in a rage, learn to internalise these emotions. In the majority of cases, good anger management will result in a positive outcome.

You may be cross with someone for something they did wrong but if you think about it long enough, you will most likely find that it was the *action* that made you angry and not the *person*. On far too many occasions, we blame the person instead of the action resulting in the mistake.

Expand your horizons.

Try to learn something new (out of your comfort zone) every month, no matter how small. This will increase your sense of accomplishment and self-belief.

Another two important things that the power of believing in yourself will achieve, is to intensify your self-confidence and remove your fears.

You have to understand that personal insecurity and low self-esteem are not conditions, they are the result of a choice. If you choose not to believe in yourself, you *will* end up with a low self-esteem.

Choose better; choose the high road; choose to be self-assured and to be positive about your future. Only you can shape the outcome of your life.

If you keep on telling yourself that you are going to fail, you will. If you keep on choosing an ordinary path, you will end up being just that: ordinary.

Sometimes life can get a little chaotic. We have work, children, parents, other relationships, more work, demands, financial stress… all of them just pile up after a while.

Don't let that get you under. Breathe and then take a step backwards to re-evaluate and reprioritise your life. You can do this. You are the ruler of your own life because you believe in yourself.

Other than the guidelines I have provided up to now, the Dalai Lama has come up with ten rules of life, all of which will also assist you in succeeding while on your path to greatness.

Here they are (with some comments):

1. Take into account that great love and great achievements involve great risk.

This does not mean the risk will automatically realise, but be prepared for it and plan ahead.

2. When you lose, don't lose the lesson.

We all make mistakes, but learn from them. Everything can be a lesson if you know how to listen to it.

3. Remember that not getting what you want is sometimes a wonderful stroke of luck.

You might just find another door right next to the one that got slammed shut in your face. This second door might lead to a treasure room filled with gold.

4. Judge your success by what you had to give up in order to get it.

We sacrifice a lot of things and we work very hard to reach our goals. Make sure they are worth it.

5. Do not let a little dispute injure a great friendship.

We all have times when we argue with other people, but you have to watch what you say during these fights. You might just hurt someone's feelings unnecessarily.

6. When you realise you've made a mistake, take immediate steps to correct it.

Correcting these mistakes should be used as an opportunity to improve your character and grow stronger.

7. Spend some alone time every day.

Use your twenty minutes each morning to reflect on your life, your goals and your dreams.

8. Open your arms to change, but do not let go of your values.

Values such as respect, truth, responsibility and gratitude shouldn't be compromised when you seize opportunities coming your way.

9. Remember that silence is sometimes the best answer.

If you don't have anything nice to say, don't say it at all, even if it is the hardest thing to do.

10. A loving atmosphere in your home is the foundation for your life.

If you disagree with your family, talk it out in the present and find a peaceful solution before you go to bed or into the next day.

* * *

I want to talk about the word, karma, quickly (if you're not a fan of the word, please feel free to replace it with "energy").

We don't have to worry about enforcing any rules in life. We obviously have to abide by the rules, but we do not have to enforce them – that is a job for the authorities.

I see karma as an energy shield that protects us in human society. It is an energy that will return to you. If you do good, you will create good karma and good things will come back to you, like in the case of Billy Harris (Remember him? The homeless man who had kept the lady's engagement ring for her, after it had slipped off her finger into his cup with coins).

But, if you start to rip off other people, you will create a bad energy field that will come back to haunt you at a later stage.

I once did a proposal for a potential client and it took me a month to complete. I provided detailed costing outlines, creative concepts, ideas and even a location for a launch.

This client's new marketing manager then appointed one of his friends, who used my proposal as a stolen idea to conduct their own marketing campaign.

At first, I felt cheated and couldn't believe what they had done, but then I realised I didn't have to worry about the problem. Somewhere along the line, the negative energy these guys had created would eventually return to them.

Instead of fighting fire with fire, I always say: fight fire with water (which makes more logical sense in any event). Feel sorry for these people and send them love; they are going to need it, believe me.

Fighting fire with water will allow you to rise above the negative energy or karma created by someone else. You do not want to lower yourself to those negative energy levels.

Remember: retaliation rarely works for the better in life.

Another good example of this concept is when you are having a fight with someone. If they raise their voice, it doesn't help for you to raise your voice as well.

All that is going to happen is it will end up in a loud screaming match and nothing much will be achieved.

Rather say something like: "I can see that you are really upset at the moment, but let us calm down and talk about this later in a sensible way, please?"

* * *

Another quality that is particularly helpful on your path to greatness is self-awareness.

Each of us has certain motivators that drive us to take action every day. Become acutely aware of them and realise how they are affecting your unique personality.

These motivators are things that really matter to us and encourage us. Getting to understand them, along with being aware of who you are and what you want to achieve, will assist you in finding the route you need to follow to fulfil your vision and discover true happiness.

Chasing your dreams through good and crystal clear self-awareness is the very first step to living the life you have always wanted to live.

Having a good sense of self-awareness will also create a balance between your personal, social and professional goals.

When asked what he thought to be the secret to success, Novak Djokovic answered, "While chasing goals on the court, don't forget to build yourself up as a human being. Life as an athlete is wonderful and adventurous, but it doesn't last forever. That is why it is important to grow in every aspect of your life and invest in your knowledge and confidence outside the court. Being a champion means mastering both work and private life, and that is not always easy. I am always on the lookout for new knowledge and new inspiration."

A key success factor on your journey is having a balanced lifestyle. This will set off a sense of harmony and fulfilment in your mind and will add meaning to your life.

First write down all the things that you need perform the balancing act on (in no particular order):

- Work, school, university
- Hobbies
- Love life
- Friends
- Relaxation
- Family, children, parents
- Physical exercise
- Spirituality
- Health

Now begin to prioritise and allocate time slots to each one of these items. Generate a schedule and fill it first with things that you *have* to do.

For instance, you have to go to work every day from a certain time in the morning until a certain time in the afternoon. If you don't, you won't have an income and therefore will not be able to spend time on stuff like hobbies anyway.

Then slot in the other activities before and after work and on weekends. Here you might have to compromise; there are only so many hours in a week.

In certain instances, two or three of the items on your list can be combined together. If you enjoy riding a bicycle, for example, you can go for a ride every afternoon after work, thereby taking care of physical exercise, a hobby, as well as your health. You can go even one step further and ride to work on your bicycle every Friday, thereby throwing in a fourth item into your balancing act.

Be creative, but be sure to maintain a balanced lifestyle. You will experience less stress and, once you have created a schedule, you will actually find that you have more time on your hands than you originally anticipated.

* * *

When things get in your way and you become frustrated, thinking, *why is it taking so long to achieve my goals*? don't turn into your own worst enemy by comparing yourself to others.

Be kind to yourself and encourage yourself to keep calm and keep on believing. Everything happens in the way it does for a very specific reason.

You might look around and see other people reaching their dreams faster than you are. Don't make the mistake of trying to match what they are doing; you are running your own race. You are not racing against other people, so do not fall into the trap of trying to chase them. Keep on chasing your *own* goals in life and be yourself.

The moment you realise that there is no competition, you will find that it becomes easier to achieve your milestones and easier to process failures along the way. Your morale will be lifted and your mindset will be focused on your *own* race.

One of the clients I worked for in New York - a watch brand - had Cindy Crawford as its ambassador. She was told by many modelling agencies in her young days that she had to remove the mole on her face. But Cindy decided: *No, this is me, I am going to make this part of my own look.* She was running her own race and made a success from it.

* * *

A few last thoughts about living the life you have always dreamed of:

- Eat healthy. Food for the body is also food for the mind and the soul.
- Drink lots of water. Many of us are so busy drinking cool drinks, hot drinks and other forms of liquids that we forget that pure water will cleanse waste in your body.
- Exercise, exercise, exercise. Enough said.
- Smile more often and laugh more often. It's good for your spirit and can change a bad mood into an excellent one.

- If you are a coffee drinker, try to cut down on the caffeine. Although it may seem to clear your mind, it's unhealthy and makes you jittery. Either keep it down to one cup a day or try caffeine-free coffee.
- Sing. It makes you feel happy.
- Do not watch too much television. Before this invention, people were more creative with their hands and spent more time with each other.
- Congratulate people around you when they achieve something significant. They will appreciate it more than you'll ever know.
- Stop complaining. Dr. Michael Merzenich, one of the world's most renowned neuroscientists, proved that constant complaining changes your brain for the worse. When we repeatedly focus on the negative by complaining, we are firing and re-firing the neurons responsible for the negativity bias.
- Drive carefully. Traffic accidents are the number one unnatural cause of death (and the only non-disease related one on the World Health Organisation's top causes of fatalities list)
- Sleep enough. Your mind and body cannot operate without a daily recharge of their batteries.

Now, open yourself up to the incredible positive change you are about to inflict on your life.

There are just way too many people living colourless lives all around us.

We only have one life on earth. Let's make it special; let's make it unforgettable.

Tell yourself: “I can and I will.”

CHAPTER 13

Plan B?

So, you have followed all the guidelines discussed up to this point and you have finally achieved some of your goals. Then, seemingly out of nowhere, something happens and the house of cards collapses spectacularly. Your very first question might be: *Why didn't I have a plan B*?

The answer is a little complicated, because there won't really be a plan B in chasing your dreams. This is an ongoing process and it is impossible to plan for unforeseen events.

Let me explain it by means of an example:

Imagine there is a man – let's name him Bob – living on a piece of land in the Indian Ocean, called Fantasy Island.

Bob has an ordinary life, working as an admin clerk at the island's immigration office. He has a wife and two sons, four and six years old respectively. They live in a small house in the centre of the island and Bob is not happy with his life. He is slightly overweight, his house is far from what he would call a dream home and he earns a mediocre salary at his immigration job.

On Bob's thirty-fourth birthday, his wife gives him a motivational book as a present.

Bob reads the book and decides to turn his ordinary life around and to become something great. He creates a vision board and writes down his goals:

- Become fit and get a six-pack: 8 months from today
- Quit my job and become a successful stockbroker: 3 years from today
- Enrol our kids into the most prestigious private school on the island: 18 months from today
- Buy a three-storey beach house and live next to the ocean: 5 years from today
- Take my family on a European vacation: 6 years from today

Now, let us fast forward six years.

Bob is forty years old and in better physical shape than ever. He is also making tons of money on the stock exchange. He is living in a beautiful beach house and the kids are delighted with the private school they now attend.

While the family is on holiday in Europe, something terrible happens on Fantasy Island: in some of the coastal areas, including Bob's neighbourhood, a chemical solution from carbonate rocks causes a collapse of the ground's surface layer. This produces a number of sinkholes to be fixed by the government.

Upon returning, Bob finds several disturbing realities.

His beach house is flattened to the ground, the children's school buildings are gone and – although the stock markets are still intact

– the local currency, *Fantasia*, had plummeted to 27*F* to the US Dollar. Devastated, he realises he will have to start everything from scratch. *I didn't have a plan B*, he tells himself.

What could Bob have done differently?

Not much really.

He could perhaps have applied the age-old saying, "Don't put all your eggs in one basket" by not buying a three-storey beach house, perhaps purchasing a double-storey instead and then a second, smaller flat higher up in the mountains. Or he could have given up on one of his dreams and built his three-storey mansion up in the mountains.

However, those changes aren't really constituting a plan B. It's more of a fallback contingency or a risk management plan. You see, if Bob had property up in the mountains, a bush fire could have destroyed it instead of a sinkhole.

The point here is that you cannot spend your life planning around *potential* unforeseen circumstances. Most of the time, this type of planning becomes negative and will hinder your progress and drain your valuable energy.

You have to take what is thrown at you, as and when it comes. Unfortunately, there is no pre-defined protocol for natural disasters or any other unexpected catastrophes.

On most occasions there is no silver bullet to prevent these events from happening. You will have to deal with them as they present themselves (more often than not when you least expect them).

Identify the potential risks and monitor them, but manage them only once they realise.

So, what happens to our poor Bob then?

Well, he has read the motivational book and he believes in himself unconditionally.

The first thing he does is to take a deep breath. Then he stands back and tells his family: "Look, there is nothing we can do about the past. We have to focus on our future. Let us accept our current situation and move forward from here."

He creates a new vision board and follows his goals and milestones in order to chase his new dreams.

They live in a shelter for sinkhole victims for a few weeks, while Bob frees up some of his stocks, and then they begin to build their dream house again; this time less spectacular but much more homely and more cosy. They use the opportunity to improve on some of the mistakes they had made in the past.

The kids attend the temporary school down at the beach and they are happy, since all the other kids also come from families who are recovering from the disaster.

Bob will go on to succeed again, because he believes in himself and because he has a positive mindset. He has skilled himself in the art of achieving goals.

The bottom line is: you cannot plan for something that *could perhaps* occur. It will clutter your vision and put unnecessary stress on your mood.

There is no plan B. It is something that will throw you off track. You only have one life.

Another example of how a plan B can hinder your progress is when you want to learn a new language.

You decide on Spanish and, based on your extensive research, you buy an audio book to learn the language. However, as a plan B, you fire up *Netflix* and start to watch native Mexican movies. Because you are a big fan of movies, you end up watching more Mexican films than actually listening to your audio book.

Sure, you learn the language, but the Spanish dialect in Mexico is completely different to the one in Spain. When you arrive in Madrid, nobody understands you because of your Mexican accent.

Plan your life as if everything is going to work out fine. If it doesn't, take a breath, accept your new situation and recalibrate your expectations.

Then start with a new vision and create new goals. You can do this because you believe in yourself. Tell life to bring on the curveballs; you can handle them. You have done it before and you can do it again.

Persist and you will come out on top.

* * *

The legendary singer and songwriter, Bob Marley, had this idea; it was kind of a virologist's idea. He believed that you could cure racism and hate by injecting music and love into people's lives.

At a stage in his career, he was scheduled to perform at a peace rally in Jamaica. Gunmen came to his house before the show and shot him down. Two days later he walked out on that stage and sang. When somebody asked him afterwards why he wasn't at home, recovering, he said, "The people who are trying to make this world worse are not taking a day off. How can I?"

That is the type of perseverance that will help you deal with the setbacks life sometimes brings across your path.

Perseverance is about developing an ability to deal with obstacles on your journey. It is a blend of mindset and habit.

It's about having the strength to keep on going and moving forward. In your mind, it's about realising what to do and how to cope with setbacks without becoming frustrated or giving up. Perseverance will allow you to go forward in life longer, harder, faster and smarter.

I know it is very difficult to stay persistent while you are in agony or upset. But believing in yourself and believing in your dreams will make this a little easier.

If you can vividly see your vision, the perseverance to achieve success will naturally come to you.

Persistent people have the mindset and vigour to keep them motivated through the tough times. Persistent people have the skills to adapt to new baselines and amend their milestones accordingly.

Stay strong after the setbacks in your life and keep on adopting the mindset of: *It can only go better from here and into the future.*

The sooner you accept that you are now working from a new baseline, the sooner your vision will begin to materialise.

The longer you linger in the past, the more your vision will stay words on your vision board, never to become a reality.

Although a setback will cause a delay in the process, it doesn't mean it will stop you dead in your tracks.

When you fly from one city to another and the plane has to turn around at some point due to inclement weather, it doesn't mean you will *never* reach your destination. It only means you are going to reach your destination a bit *later*.

And later isn't always all that bad. It gives you more time for self-reflection.

Rome wasn't built in a day and no great sustainable success has ever been achieved by luck. They have been achieved by persistence and hard work. You can clean leaves from a pool every autumn afternoon and the following morning they will be back. If you don't persist, they will, and you will lose the battle. Never underestimate the power of persistence. It ensures a positive mindset and strengthens your character.

* * *

Sometimes, setbacks in your life will make you feel as if the whole world is against you. Do not allow these feelings to get you under and do not give up hope. Tomorrow is a new day and the sun will come up just as it did yesterday and today.

Regroup, rebuild and define your new targets.

There are people who say, "What do I do now?" and there are people who say, "I know I can make this work."

Become part of the latter group.

While there is no plan B when it comes to chasing your dreams, there are a few checks and balances you can put in place to stack the deck of cards more in your favour:

- Identify risks and monitor them
- Watch out for volatile external factors
- Don't put all your eggs in one basket
- Reflect more often where risks are involved
- Never become discouraged by setbacks; see them as opportunities to learn and improve

You can do anything.

Just believe.

* * *

Calmness can assist you a great deal.

Once you have experienced a setback and you start to panic you won't achieve a lot. If you stay calm, on the other hand, it will allow you to breathe and re-assess your new position with a clear mind.

You will be able to diffuse tense situations and make better decisions. A calm attitude slows down your heart rate, opens up your subconscious to new ideas and helps you to think logically.

Calmness will also help you to develop two other important skills: patience and optimism. Both of these are key in surviving during a pressure situation.

If you struggle to stay calm through setbacks, use your support network. Delegate some of the crisis management steps to them.

Because they believe in you, they will be glad to take some weight off your shoulders.

This will allow you to focus on what you can control instead of running around and achieving very little because you are fighting too many fires at the same time.

* * *

There are some real statements out there that were made by people who lived many years ago and that were at the time believed to be the absolute truth.

Here are some of them:

“Whoever travels at a speed of thirty miles per hour or more will most certainly suffocate and die.” (year: 1840)

“There is no possible combination that can be put together in a machine that can ever help people to fly.” (year: 1901)

“Travelling to the moon is a stupid idea and is impossible.” (year: 1926)

“It is impossible to make use of the energy that is stored in matter.” (year: 1930)

Those were not only statements made by people who believed in them, but they were common beliefs among all humanity during these times.

They were believed to be mere fantasies; impossible fantasies, people called them back then.

How can you also achieve the impossible?

Well, for us who are now living in the twenty-first century, those statements appear to be absurd because they had all been proven wrong already.

Today, travelling at a speed of thirty miles is considered fairly slow, unless you are riding a bicycle. Airplanes are flying around in the sky every single day. The Americans already went to the moon, while power plants with reactors that can extract energy out of physical matter can be seen in many countries.

How did it then transpire that some of these seemingly impossible "fantasies" were proven wrong later?

The answer is simple.

People like the Wright Brothers, Albert Einstein, Thomas Edison and Louis Pasteur simply refused to accept the concept of impossible.

They ignored the naysayers and persisted in chasing their goals. The Wrights eventually built the world's very first airplane, Einstein developed the theory of relativity and quantum mechanics, Edison mastered the lightbulb and the motion picture camera, while Pasteur pioneered the principles of vaccination.

You, too, can invent your light bulb or your airplane.

Convince yourself that you have the ability to make the impossible possible. Then visualise it by playing that movie in your head, where you see yourself doing it.

In order to do this, the two critical ingredients are self-belief and perseverance. Self-belief will keep you confident, inspired and motivated, while perseverance will increase your chances of success and help you to learn from previous mistakes or failures.

Refuse to accept the limitations other people are trying to impose upon you and chase your goals with vigour.

Refuse to admit to the existence of impossibilities. Just because you couldn't do something the first or the second time doesn't make it impossible.

Try again and again until you succeed.

Time will bring you your reward and you will finally conquer.

Colonel Sanders travelled all over the United States to get someone to sell his fried chicken, made with his secret herbs and spices recipe. He was rejected over a thousand times, when he finally struck a deal in Utah.

Sanders kept his cool and didn't go into a blind panic after one thousand rejections (that's two rejections a day for more than a year and a half). The ever-persistent Colonel was sixty-five years old when Kentucky Fried Chicken – today one of the world's most recognisable brands – was born.

Never give up. Ever.

Have you ever watched waves crushing down onto the rocks on a stormy day? They are relentless and never-ending. Be the same: become relentless and never stop reaching for your dreams.

Madonna dropped out of a university dance scholarship and moved to New York City with only $35 in her pocket.

Later, she told people that it was the bravest thing she had ever done in her life.

She began working as a backup singer for other bands, then started her own bands and eventually became one of the most popular solo artists of all time.

Madonna was persistent, ruthless, and not only did she have musical talent, she had a talent for working hard.

Become one of those people who can make the impossible possible.

Nelson Mandela was in prison for twenty-seven years and then went on to become the president of his country.

Nothing is impossible.

Whatever you can imagine, you can achieve in life.

Just believe.

Start believing now

Y

ou wake up one Saturday morning, thinking to yourself: *Today is going to be greatest day of my life!*

The early summer sun is bathing your bedroom in a golden glow, the smell of freshly mowed lawns fills your senses, the sound of children laughing in the park rings in your ears and a beautiful yellow-and-black bird is perched on the windowsill outside your bedroom.

You take a deep breath of fresh air and start to play the day's movie in your head.

It's an awesome movie. Everything is going to go according to plan and the day is going to end in success and happiness.

You climb out of bed and look at yourself in the mirror.

You are in tip-top condition! your mind tells you. *Keep it up; a healthy body hosts a healthy mind.*

Since you are going to seize the day, you dress in your favourite t-shirt, a pair of comfortable shorts and your ultra-light running shoes.

You check your vision board and remind yourself of the dreams you still want to achieve.

What an exciting life I'm living! you think, walking to the kitchen to drink a glass of cool celery juice.

Pulling back your shoulders and lifting your head up high, you go outside for an early morning jog. You feel refreshed, relaxed and invigorated.

While running down the street, you think, *I am so grateful to be alive and for my senses, to take in all the beauty of Mother earth.*

Back home, you drink some mineral water and wipe your face with a soft towel. Then you leave your cell phone in the kitchen and go out into the garden to take a twenty-minute timeout to reflect on what you have achieved this week.

It's incredible – even more than you have planned for.

After your timeout, you check your Facebook page, where you posted the following feed yesterday:

A year from now I am in the Big Apple! Yay!

Underneath your post, the latest comment (by a person who always tells you that you cannot live the life you want to) is the following:

Yeah, let me know how that works out for you, buddy.

You ignore the comment and smile brightly. Below the naysayer's comment there are thirty-four likes from people encouraging you:

Go for it! You can do anything my friend.
Can't wait to see the pics!

You're an absolute star! I admire your bravery.

These are comments from all the people in your success network and your extended support structure; your family, your sidekick, your mentors and your connectors.

You have involved them in your goal to go to New York City to start your career. It is something you have wanted to do since you graduated from university.

While scrolling down the page, your eyes fall on an advertisement calling on members of the community to please assist the homeless shelter down the street by donating blankets, tinned food and long-life milk.

You make a mental note of the address and start scavenging for food and sauces in the pantry. You are surprised by how many things are in there that are still perfectly fine, although your family and you hardly ever use them or eat them.

In the end, you are able to fill eight shopping bags with supplies and it feels good to know that you are giving something back to society.

A feeling of positive energy rushes through your body while your daily movie plays on in your mind.

The picture is clear:

After you drop off the supplies at the homeless shelter, you are going to clean out your garage (*Maybe I'll find more stuff I can give away)* and then paint the walls in a bright green. It will make the place lively and give it a clean and fresh appearance.

At noon you are going on a family picnic in the park and that's going to be an adventure of note. You haven't seen some of your cousins in months. Besides, at this time of the year, the park is filled with birds, bunnies and thousands of butterflies; something to behold.

This evening you need to get a proposal done for work (*Shouldn't take more than two hours*) and then you are taking the love of your life to a quiet little restaurant that has a special on seafood. Perhaps you will order a bottle of sparkling wine to celebrate the incredible sales deal you've landed earlier in the week.

Finally, you are going to lay your head down on your pillow and dream about more magnificent adventures – at work, in your personal life, and in everything you do to make the world a better place

Yes, today is going to be a marvellous day, you think, staring at the clock against the wall.

Not even nine o'clock in the morning yet…

The whole relaxing Saturday in front of me. I am going to seize it and turn it upside down!

How blessed am I for such a wonderful life?

I am living the life I have always wanted to live and I am eternally grateful for that.

And I believe I can achieve so much more.

Watch out world, here I come!

Because I believe…

* * *

What's next?

Continue with your journey to success and keep in touch. Tell me how well you are succeeding.

You can find me here:

https://www.believeadvertising.com/
https://www.facebook.com/BelieveAdvertising/
https://www.instagram.com/believeadvertising/
afalk@believeadvertising.com

BELIEVE!

AND IT WILL HAPPEN.

Many Thanks

I am so grateful for the people below who have come into my life for a reason, season or a lifetime. Thank you for all of your support. Especially thanks to:

Michelle Falk – my amazing wife for your guidance and for being there for me.

Gisele & Eden – I love you until eternity and thank you for your unconditional love.

My parents – thanks for always caring for me and worrying about me and bringing me into this world.

My sisters – thanks for always laughing at my jokes and looking out for me.

The Goodman's – you are the best in-laws anyone could ask for.

My brothers and sisters in-law – I know you all think I'm a little wacky, and guess what, you're right! Thanks for loving me like your own sibling.

The Goodwin family – you all are like my second family.

Erik Dochtermann, Margie Cooper, Jennifer Jones & the KD&E gang. You answered my email back in 1997 from a young Aussie (yes we have computers and speak English down here!) who wanted to take the word by storm. I am forever thankful for you believing in me.

Chris Chamberlin – I still can't believe you aren't with us anymore but know you are looking down on us all with a glass of champers.

Charlotte Varey, Steven Lalic, Tal Bloom, Heidi Klaesi & Yvonne Kerr– thanks for being there from day one of Believe Advertising and for your ongoing support.

Jonathan Goddard – thanks for bringing the excitement of New York into my Sydney life.

Julian Moss, Simon Sibia & Ben Anderson – You guys trusted me with your vodka brand and what a success it became. Working with you over the past decade was so much fun. Thank you for letting me roll with my crazy vodka parties that put Vodka O on the map.

My Believe dream team – thank you for always giving your all, each day.

My previous, current, and future clients – thank you so much for believing in me and entrusting me with your business. I am really lucky that I love what I do each and every day.

And you! Thanks for reading my story and for your time. I really hope I have inspired you to make a difference in your life while making a difference in the world.

Sources/References:

- 365 Days of Positive Thinking - Jenny Kellett - 2016
- Carve your destiny (motion picture) - Anubhav Srivastava - 2015
- Everything I Never Told You - Celeste Ng - 2015
- Feel the fear and do it anyway - *How to turn your fear and indecision into confidence and action* - Susan Jeffers - 1988
- How to See Yourself As You Really Are - Dalai Lama XIV – 2008
- I am Legend, (motion picture) – Mark Protosevich, Akiva Goldsman (2007)
- https://beinspiredchannel.com/dalai-lama-motivational
- https://dowsers.com/dr-masaru-emotos-messages-from-water
- https://fractalenlightenment.com/33936/life/how-your-thoughts-become-your-destiny
- https://liberationist.org
- https://novakdjokovicfoundation.org/10-tips-from-novak-djokovic-on-how-to-achieve-success
- Know Yourself - A Book of Questions - Irene Smit, Astrid Van Der Hulst - 2018
- Today News - Man who returned ring no longer homeless - Lilit Marcus - 2013
- Mastering Your Thoughts - Olu David - 2010
- Sapiens (A Brief History of Humankind) - Yuval Noah Harari - 2014
- Self-Reflection Questions for Introspection - Courtney Ackerman - 2017

- SUCCESS Magazine - How to Train Your Brain for Positive Thinking - Brendon Burchard - 2017
- The Energy Bus - Jon Gordon - 2007
- The Entrepreneur playing the PR game - Tasnuva Bindi - Apr 2013
- The power of others (Why Your Success Depends on The Strength of Your Relationships) - Gustavo Razzetti - 2018
- The rules of life - Richard Templar - 2010
- What we ache for - Oriah Mountain Dreamer - 1993
- www.brainyquote.com
- www.entrepreneur.com/article/254562
- www.goalcast.com/2017/03/20/top-20-inspiring-mahatma-gandhi-quotes
- www.goodlifeproject.com
- www.iol.co.za
- www.mind-your-reality.com/thought_power.html
- www.participatorymethods.org/method/reflective-practice
- www.powerofpositivity.com
- www.willnevergiveup.com/madonna-never-gave

About the Author

Founder of Believe Advertising and PR, Adrian Falk, has been successfully generating national and international press coverage for clients for over 17 years.

Adrian has worked with a diverse range of lifestyle, beauty and fashion clients, including SEIKO, Furla, VDKA 6100, and has worked on many high profile PR campaigns, including the international PR campaign with Novak Djokovic for the worldwide launch of HEAD's new Graphene Speed tennis racquet, and the international press conference announcing SEIKO's partnership with Novak Djokovic.

From supporting local schools in Fiji with laptop computers to providing 240 meals to school children in India, 3,650 days' worth of grain seeds to nourish hungry youth in Malawi, and helped give

361 days of access to lighting for underprivileged families, Adrian is all about giving back so that he can leave the world a better place than when he found it.

Made in the USA
Coppell, TX
10 July 2020

30593769R00098